TODAY'S EVERYDAY
SLOW
COOKER

TODAY'S EVERYDAY
SLOW COOKER

100 EASY & DELICIOUS RECIPES

DONNA-MARIE PYE

Robert
ROSE

For Lawrence, Darcy and Jack

You were my inspiration for many of the recipes so many years ago, and the reason I still continue to love to cook. Our time in the kitchen and meals around the table are my happiest memories of all.

• •

Today's Everyday Slow Cooker
Text copyright © 2021 Donna-Marie Pye
Photography copyright © gettyimages.com & istockphoto.com
Cover and text design copyright © 2021 Robert Rose Inc.

For complete cataloging information, see page 192.

Disclaimer
The recipes in this book have been carefully tested by our kitchen and our tasters. To the best of our knowledge, they are safe and nutritious for ordinary use and users. For those people with food or other allergies, or who have special food requirements or health issues, please read the suggested contents of each recipe carefully and determine whether or not they may create a problem for you. All recipes are used at the risk of the consumer.

We cannot be responsible for any hazards, loss or damage that may occur as a result of any recipe use.

For those with special needs, allergies, requirements or health problems, in the event of any doubt, please contact your medical adviser prior to the use of any recipe.

At the time of publication, all URLs referenced link to existing websites. Robert Rose Inc. is not responsible for maintaining, and does not endorse the content of, any website or content not created by Robert Rose Inc.

DESIGN AND PRODUCTION: Kevin Cockburn/PageWave Graphics Inc.
EDITOR: Christine Sanger
PROOFREADER: Meredith Dees
INDEXER: Gillian Watts

The publisher gratefully acknowledges the financial support of our publishing program by the Government of Canada through the Canada Book Fund.

Canadä

Published by Robert Rose Inc.
120 Eglinton Avenue East, Suite 800, Toronto, Ontario, Canada M4P 1E2
Tel: (416) 322-6552 Fax: (416) 322-6936
www.robertrose.ca

Printed and bound in South Korea

1 2 3 4 5 6 7 8 9 FC 29 28 27 26 25 24 23 22 21

CONTENTS

INTRODUCTION

The conversation started innocently like this: "Donna-Marie, I am thinking about re-launching a slow cooker cookbook and I was wondering what you'd think about it." These were the words from my publisher early in January 2020. It's been more than 10 years since we published any new material, and a lot has changed in the world of slow cooking. New appliances for cooking whole meals have arrived in the marketplace, plant-based eating has become a common practice, and many people are faced with dietary restrictions such as low carb, gluten- and dairy-free just to name a few. There are thousands of recipes available online, and today's savvy cooks turn to many sources for recipe ideas. Still, the opportunity to relaunch recipes to a new generation of cooks intrigued me and of course my answer was "Yes, let's do it."

My relationship with the slow cooker began many years ago when I was in university and then became a commuter to my first job located an hour from my home. Once I married, then became a mother with young children, my life reached a new level of busyness. Today I run my own cooking school and kitchen retail store, my children are grown and living on their own (or at least one of them is) and yet I still find myself using my slow cooker at least once a week. It gives me a chance to come home at the end of the day and sit down with my husband and son and not have to think "What am I cooking for dinner tonight?"

Slow cookers are a breeze to use and are time-, cost- and energy-efficient. Stalwart and reliable, they require little or no tending, and very little last-minute cooking is needed. Meats and poultry braise beautifully, resulting in exceptional pot roasts, savory stews, and succulent ribs, chilies and curries. Beans, peas and lentils — which are inexpensive, filling and incredibly nutritious — benefit from long slow cooking. Slow cookers also offer a heat-free way to cook in the summer.

I developed these recipes with convenience in mind, while also being conscious of the way we eat today. While some recipes require a few extra minutes of preparation, in many cases you can add the ingredients in all at once. I try to use mostly fresh ingredients, but I dip into the pantry from time to time. You'll notice more contemporary ingredients, such as chipotle peppers, smoked paprika and tahini to reflect current cooking styles and global influence.

Slow cooking has evolved significantly over the years and is now more sophisticated and encompasses a wider variety of flavors, cuisine styles, shapes and textures. So, whether you're cooking for a family or just a few people, this book makes easy work of creating delicious, soul-satisfying meals. Happy slow cooking!

PARTS OF A SLOW COOKER

These sleek countertop appliances have some key parts, and different models offer different features. Before buying a slow cooker, you'll want to consider all of the options and decide on the model that best meets your budget and household requirements.

CASING AND INSERT

The appliance consists of a metal outer casing and a stoneware insert. Some stoneware is designed so that you can use it to brown meat or sauté vegetables on the stovetop before placing it in the metal casing for slow cooking. But check your manufacturer's instructions to see whether this is possible with your model. If not, it's just as easy to do your browning or sautéing in a skillet, then transfer the food to the stoneware. The recipes in this book assume the use of a skillet.

The metal casing contains thermostatically controlled heating elements, which heat up to warm the air inside the insulated metal walls, thereby cooking the meal. This low-wattage heat never makes direct contact with the stoneware, so there are no hot spots and no need for constant stirring. The slow cooker uses about the same amount of energy as a 100-watt light bulb — substantially less than a conventional oven.

If your stoneware insert is removable, the manufacturer's directions will specify whether it is ovenproof, microwaveable and/or able to go under the broiler.

LID

All slow cookers come with a plastic or glass lid. A good lid seals in moisture and nutrients, so, while a little jiggle is acceptable, you will want to make sure the lid fits snugly. Clear lids are handy, as they allow you to see what is happening inside the slow cooker. Tempting as it might seem, it is important not to lift the lid during cooking — you can lose 20 minutes of cooking time for every lift. Look for lids that are dishwasher-safe. I have had some heat-resistant plastic ones that started out clear but with time and continued washing became opaque, making it difficult to see what was happening inside.

Glass lids get quite hot during the cooking process. When it's time to remove the lid, it's a good idea to use oven mitts or a pot holder.

TIMER AND TEMPERATURE PROBE

Many of today's slow cookers come with a programmable timer. Some of these allow you to use preset times within the High or Low settings; others allow you to set the cooking time, then choose whether to cook on High or Low. Many machines have a Warm setting, which will kick in automatically once the preset cooking time is reached, keeping the contents warm without overcooking them. If the food is forgiving, the Warm setting can also be handy when you're taking cooked food to a potluck. Transport the food in your slow cooker and, once you reach your destination, turn on the Warm setting; the food can safely sit that way for up to 2 hours.

Some slow cookers are also equipped with a temperature probe, which works with the cooker's electronic controls to monitor the internal temperature of meat and automatically shifts to the Warm setting when the desired temperature is reached. Internal temperature is the best way to measure the doneness of some types of meats and poultry, and the probe ensures that these meats are thoroughly cooked according to specified guidelines.

The most basic machines do not have features such as a programmable timer or a temperature probe. Before buying one, do make sure it at least has High and Low settings; otherwise, it cannot be considered a true slow cooker.

SIZE AND SHAPE

Slow cookers come in an impressive range of sizes and shapes. Choose one that is best suited to your needs. You'd be surprised at how many households own two — one for large family meals and another for cooking side dishes, desserts and appetizers.

If you plan to make 4 to 8 servings most of the time, a 4- to 6-quart (4 to 6 L) slow cooker is the best size for you. This capacity will allow you to cook a full meal with leftovers (depending on how hungry everyone is). Most of the recipes in this book were tested in a slow cooker this size. Smaller models, in the $1\frac{1}{2}$- to 3-quart (1.5 to 3 L) range, are ideal for smaller households, and for making warm dips, side dishes and appetizers for which a large pot is simply too big. If you regularly (or even occasionally) feed a crowd, or you simply like to make big batches and freeze your leftovers, you may want to invest in a 6- to 7-quart (6 to 7 L) slow cooker, which is capable of making up to 20 servings.

Slow cookers come in round, oval and rectangular models. While round slow cookers are fine for soups, stews and chilies, oval and rectangular models allow a little more flexibility when it comes to roasts and larger cuts of meat. A rectangular shape also makes more efficient use of cupboard space.

The amount of liquid in a recipe can vary considerably, from just a few spoonfuls to enough to submerge the food completely. Ideally, the slow cooker should be no more than two-thirds full of food, with liquid at least 1 inch (2.5 cm) from the rim.

HANDLES, FEET AND CORD STORAGE

Slow cookers are popular as tote-along appliances when potluck is the name of the game. Look for easy-to-grip handles that can be grasped with oven mitts on. The stoneware handles heat up when the appliance is cooking, so make sure to protect your hands accordingly.

Because slow cookers can heat up kitchen counters, many people worry about possible heat damage or even fire risk. It is always best to place your slow cooker on a solid, heat-resistant surface. However, to alleviate this problem, some manufacturers have developed slow cookers that have feet, or bases with rubberized bottoms. This feature makes using a slow cooker worry-free.

Finally, some manufacturers have developed retractable electric cords that store conveniently and efficiently inside the base of the slow cooker — a very helpful feature when storage space is at a premium.

When cleaning the slow cooker, never immerse the metal housing in water. It only needs a gentle wipe with a damp cloth to remove any dribbles or stickiness. Dry it with a clean kitchen towel so as not to damage the finish.

8 ESSENTIAL TRICKS OF THE TRADE

Your slow cooker can be used to create any dish! Here are my top 8 tips to help you use your appliance to its full advantage.

1 | Prepare What You Can Ahead of Time

If you plan to start your slow cooker early in the day, here are a few things you can prepare the night before:

- Chop fresh vegetables, place them in airtight containers and refrigerate until the next day. Vegetables that will be used at the same time can be put into the same container to save space.
- Defrost frozen vegetables overnight in the refrigerator.
- Trim fat from meat and poultry and remove skin from poultry. Cut meat and poultry into pieces of the same size. Cubes are the best shape for even cooking, so try to get your pieces as close to cube-shaped as possible. Do not brown meat in advance; once it's cut to size, refrigerate it in an airtight container, keeping it separate from any other ingredients. (The exception to this rule is ground meat, which can be browned the night before; however, it still needs to be refrigerated in its own container.)
- Assemble nonperishable ingredients and cooking utensils in a convenient spot for a quick start.

Recipes in this book that lend themselves to additional advance preparation or cooking are accompanied by make-ahead instructions. Many recipes can also be completely cooked in advance and stored in the refrigerator or freezer for future use.

Always read the recipe all the way through first, to make sure you have the necessary ingredients and equipment, and to get a sense of the timing and what needs to happen when.

2 | Choose Less Tender Cuts of Meat and Trim Off the Fat

The cuts of meat that benefit from slow cooking are less expensive and often from the tough shoulder area. Slow cooking breaks down the collagen in the muscles' connective tissue, leaving the meat moist and tender. Make sure to trim off all visible fat (and remove skin from poultry) before adding meat to the slow cooker. This will reduce the amount of fat you need to skim from the liquid at the end of the cooking process.

3 | Cut Root Vegetables into Small Pieces

In the slow cooker, root vegetables, such as carrots, parsnips, turnips and potatoes, take longer to cook than meat pieces of the same size, so they should be thinly sliced or cut into cubes no bigger than 1 inch (2.5 cm). It's best to place them as close as possible to the bottom and sides of the stoneware, so that they benefit from proximity to the heat source.

Because of their hard consistency, root vegetables are well suited to the slow cooker, softening slowly and releasing their natural sugars as they simmer. Softer vegetables, such as zucchini or spinach, will turn to mush if cooked for a long time; these are best added in the last 20 minutes of cooking.

4 | Brown Meat and Sauté Vegetables First

Partial cooking or browning may add a few minutes to the preparation process, but in the end, those extra minutes will be worthwhile. Browning meat not only improves its color, but also breaks down the natural sugars, releasing their flavors. Sautéing vegetables with spices and dried herbs before slow cooking produces a richer, more intense sauce.

For browning, the first step is to cut the meat or poultry into pieces of the same size. Next, dredge it in flour, coating evenly. Add it in small batches to a small amount of oil heated over medium-high heat, either in a skillet or in your stoneware if it is designed for stovetop cooking. Stir or turn frequently to brown evenly. If you are using a skillet, transfer each batch to the slow cooker as it is browned. If you're using the stoneware, remove each batch to a plate as it is browned, then return all the meat to the stoneware after deglazing.

Sauté vegetables in a small amount of oil or butter (as called for in the recipe) heated over medium-high heat in a skillet or in stovetop-safe stoneware. For recipes that also contain browned meat, sauté the vegetables after the meat, in the same pan, either with the oil that's left or with added oil or butter. You just need to soften the vegetables — they don't need to be fully cooked or browned. If you overcook them now, they'll acquire a bland flavor during slow cooking.

After browning meat or poultry and sautéing vegetables, deglaze the pan with wine or broth to release the caramelized juices created during browning. Add a small amount of the liquid to the leftover juices and cooked-on food particles in the pan, bring it to a boil, then reduce the heat and simmer for 1 to 2 minutes while scraping up the bits stuck to the bottom of the pan. Pour this aromatic liquid over the browned meat in the slow cooker to maximize the flavor in your finished dish.

Meat should be browned in small batches, no more than a single layer over the bottom of the pan. If you overcrowd the meat, it causes too much steam, lowers the temperature and leaves meat gray instead of brown.

Dredging meat or poultry in flour has a two-pronged benefit. First, it adds flavor and helps the pieces brown quickly and intensely. Second, the starch in the flour acts as a thickening agent for the cooking juices once the meat is transferred to the slow cooker.

5 | Don't Overdo the Liquids

Because moisture has no escape from the confines of the slow cooker, the amount of liquid in the stoneware increases as juices and steam are released from the food. Therefore, slow cooker recipes use only about half the liquid called for in conventional recipes. If you're new to slow cooking, keep in mind that the liquid may not cover the solids when you first add the ingredients to the slow cooker.

If you wind up with too much liquid when your meal is finished cooking, remove the lid and increase the temperature to High if necessary, then cook, uncovered, for 30 to 45 minutes to allow some liquid to evaporate.

As a general rule, the slow cooker should be no less than half full and no more than two-thirds to three-quarters full of food once all the ingredients are added.

6 | Use Whole Herbs and Spices

Whole-leaf dried herbs, such as dried thyme and oregano leaves, and whole or coarsely crushed spices release their flavor slowly throughout the long cooking process, so they are a better choice than ground herbs and spices, which tend to lose their flavor in the slow cooker. Add fresh herbs, such as basil and cilantro, during the last hour of cooking. Always taste your finished dish before serving it and adjust the salt and pepper if needed.

If you substitute fresh herbs for dried, you will need to use three times as much.

7 | Resist the Temptation to Lift the Lid

Always cook with the slow cooker lid on. The lid traps heat as it rises and converts it into steam, which is what cooks the food. Removing the lid will result in major heat loss, which the slow cooker can't quickly recover. You will need to extend the cooking time by at least 20 minutes each time you lift the lid. Do so only when it is time to check for doneness, when adding ingredients or when stirring is recommended.

If a recipe in this book instructs you to add or stir ingredients partway through, the resulting heat loss has been accounted for in the overall cooking time.

8 | Experiment with Water Baths

Delicate dishes, such as custards, puddings and cheesecakes, are cooked to perfection in a hot-water bath, or bain-marie. In conventional cooking, this technique involves setting the filled baking dish in a larger pan filled with hot water before placing it in the oven. Heat is transferred from the hot water to the dish, cooking the contents gently and slowly, so that it doesn't curdle or form a crust. The technique works wonders in the slow cooker, too: custards, puddings and cheesecakes stay creamy and smooth, and cheesecakes do not crack. The challenge, however, is finding a dish that will fit properly in the slow cooker. Standard 4-cup (1 L) or 6-cup (1.5 L) ovenproof baking bowls work well in larger slow cookers. If you are making a cheesecake, a 7-inch (18 cm) springform pan should fit nicely.

These water baths add to the heat of your dish. So that you can safely and easily remove the dish from the slow cooker, you'll want to make foil handles to place under the dish when putting it in the stoneware. Cut a 2-foot (60 cm) piece of foil in half lengthwise. Fold each strip in half lengthwise and crisscross the strips in the bottom of the stoneware, bringing the ends up to clear the rim. Place the dish in the slow cooker and pour in enough water to come 1 inch (2.5 cm) up the sides of the dish. Cover the slow cooker with its lid, making sure the ends of the foil are tucked between the rim and the lid. Use the foil handles as lifters to remove the pan from the slow cooker.

If the dish fits snugly in the slow cooker, add the water first. Since the water level will rise when you add the filled dish, test it first by pouring about 1 cup (250 mL) water into the stoneware. Add the filled pan and make sure the water rises 1 inch (2.5 cm) up the sides of the dish. If it rises any more than that, remove the pan and ladle some water out.

FOOD SAFETY CONSIDERATIONS

The U.S. Department of Agriculture assures us that, in a slow cooker that is used properly (the lid is left on and food is cooked at the appropriate heat level for the appropriate length of time), foods will reach their safe internal cooked temperature quickly enough to inhibit bacterial growth.

With that concern off the table, here are a few other kitchen safety details to consider when slow cooking:

- Always start with fresh or thawed meat and poultry. Using frozen or partially frozen meat will increase the time required for the meat's internal temperature to reach the "safe zone" in which bacteria growth is inhibited.

- In general, defrost frozen vegetables, such as peas and corn, before adding them to the slow cooker. This prevents them from slowing down the cooking process. Defrost them in the refrigerator overnight or place them under cold running water to thaw and separate.

- Cook all ground meat and ground poultry completely before adding it to the slow cooker. (There are some exceptions, and proper cooking directions are given for these in the individual recipes.) If you are cooking ground meat the night before, chill it separately from other ingredients.

- Do not refrigerate uncooked or partially cooked meat or poultry in the slow cooker stoneware, as the insert will become very cold and will slow the cooking process. Partially cook meat or poultry only when transferring it immediately to the slow cooker. Do not refrigerate for later cooking.

- Precut meats and vegetables should be stored separately in the refrigerator. After cutting uncooked meat, never use the same cutting board or knife for other foods without thoroughly washing these utensils with soap and hot water first.

- When cooking whole poultry or meatloaf, use a meat thermometer to accurately test doneness. Insert the thermometer into the thickest part of the thigh or loaf. The U.S. Department of Agriculture recommends cooking poultry and meatloaf to an internal temperature of 165°F (74°C); Health Canada recommends ensuring that the temperature has reached 170°F (77°C).

- Remove leftovers from the stoneware and refrigerate in small portions as quickly as possible.

- Do not reheat cooked food in the slow cooker. Frozen leftovers can be thawed in the refrigerator or microwave, then reheated in a conventional oven or microwave oven, or in a saucepan on the stove.

INGREDIENT ESSENTIALS

When I was developing and testing the recipes in this book, the basic ingredients I used were of standard size and consistency. The recipes make some assumptions about what is standard when it comes to basic ingredients; these distinctions are detailed below. For the best results, always use the recommended ingredient, exactly as called for, unless other options are indicated in a tip.

- When greasing stoneware, I sprayed it with nonstick cooking spray.
- Table salt is used for cooking unless otherwise indicated. Where a recipe says "season to taste," I used kosher salt.
- Dried herbs are crumbled whole leaves, not ground.
- All eggs used are large eggs; expect different results if you substitute medium or extra-large eggs. For baking recipes, eggs should be brought to room temperature before use; otherwise, they can be used directly from the refrigerator.
- I used 2% milk and yogurt unless otherwise specified.
- When sour cream is added to the slow cooker, I used 14%. If using sour cream as a topping or adding it at the end of the cooking process, you can use a lower-fat (5%) version.
- I used salted butter.
- Fresh vegetables and fruits are medium-size unless otherwise indicated. Any inedible peels, skins, seeds and cores should be removed unless otherwise indicated.
- "Onions" means regular cooking onions unless otherwise indicated.
- When I call for chopped or minced garlic, I used fresh garlic, not the preserved minced garlic available in stores.
- Canned tomatoes are diced, not whole, unless whole is specified.
- Rice is long-grain parboiled (converted), unless otherwise indicated.
- I used fresh, oven-ready lasagna noodles rather than the dried, no-boil type. For all other pasta shapes, I used dried pasta.
- Where recipes call for vegetable oil to brown meats and sauté vegetables, I used a canola/sunflower oil combination.
- When choosing poultry, look for air-chilled products, which have a firmer texture and will hold their shape better and be more tender after the long slow-cooking process.
- Avoid "seasoned" meats and poultry, which have been treated with additional water and sodium phosphate or other ingredients and tend to make slow-cooked foods watery and salty.

HOME-COOKED BEANS IN THE SLOW COOKER

The slow cooker is very useful for cooking dried beans, peas and lentils. This is great news for anyone who wants to avoid the salt and preservatives added to pre-cooked canned beans — and you'll save money by purchasing dried beans in bulk.

Transforming dried legumes into tender, edible beans, peas and lentils requires a three-step process: sorting, soaking and cooking. The cooking depends on the type of slower cooker used, the variety, age and quality of the bean, altitude and whether you use hard or soft water for cooking. The best way to test for doneness is to taste them. Cooked beans are free of any raw, starchy taste and are tender. Dried beans will more than double in size after soaking and cooking. One pound (500 g) or about 2 cups (500 mL) yields 4 to 5 cups (1 to 1.25 L) of cooked beans.

STEP 1: SORTING
Look for any damaged, broken or cracked beans and foreign material. Once sorted, place in a colander and rinse thoroughly under cold water.

STEP 2: SOAKING
Most dried beans (with the exception of lentils) must be soaked for several hours before they are cooked. This step replaces the water that was removed in the drying process, shortens the cooking time and improves the flavor, texture, appearance and digestibility of the beans. The most time-efficient method is to soak the beans overnight, then start the cooking process in the morning. Never let the beans soak for more than 18 hours. Once the soak is finished, drain the beans, discarding the liquid and rinse beans well. The beans will now be ready to cook.

- *Long Soak:* Place 1 lb (500 g) beans in slow cooker or large bowl and add 10 cups (2.5 L) boiling water. Cover and let soak for 12 hours or overnight. Drain and rinse thoroughly.

- *Quick Soak:* Place 1 lb (500 g) beans in a large saucepan or stock pot (allowing for beans to expand about two and half times the size). Add 10 cups (2.5 L) water and bring to a boil over high heat. Reduce heat and simmer for 3 minutes. Remove from heat, cover and soak for 1 hour. Drain and rinse thoroughly.

STEP 3: COOKING
Place drained, soaked beans in slow cooker. Add fresh, cold water to cover the beans ensuring water level is at least 2 inches (5 cm) above the

level of the beans. For additional flavor you can add seasonings such as a bay leaf, garlic or bouquet garni (made from fresh herbs tied together in a cheesecloth bag) to the cooking liquid. Do not add sugar, salt or acidic foods such as tomatoes as they prevent beans from softening.

Cover and cook on Low for 4 to 6 hours. Don't worry if the beans have not absorbed all the water. They should be tender, but not mushy. Drain and rinse thoroughly under cold running water. The beans are now fully cooked and recipe ready.

STORING COOKED BEANS

Once beans are completely cool, divide them into 1- or 2-cup (250 or 500 mL) portions and pack into freezer-safe containers and label portion size (since this is the amount called for in many recipes). Store in the refrigerator for up to 1 week or in the freezer for up to 3 months. Thaw beans before adding to recipes.

BREAKFASTS & BREADS

BREAKFAST OATMEAL WITH PEARS & HONEY

SERVES 4 TO 6 | 3- TO 4-QUART SLOW COOKER, STONEWARE GREASED

Shake off the night's cobwebs with a bowl of this hearty oatmeal. Steel-cut oats traditionally take a much longer time to cook than quick-cooking rolled oats do. Cooking the oatmeal overnight gives you a chance to sit down to a hot breakfast in the morning, before heading out the door.

2 cups (500 mL) steel-cut or large-flake (old-fashioned) rolled oats

¼ tsp (1 mL) ground cinnamon

4¾ cups (1.175 L) water

1 ripe pear

1 tbsp (15 mL) liquid honey

Plain yogurt (optional)

1 In prepared slow cooker stoneware, combine oats, cinnamon, and water.

2 Cover and cook on Low for 8 hours or overnight.

3 Just before serving, dice pear. Spoon oatmeal into individual serving bowls and top with diced pear. Drizzle with honey and, if desired, serve with a dollop of yogurt.

TIPS

This oatmeal dish is also great served with fresh sliced bananas or apples.

For an extra-nutty flavor, try toasting the oatmeal first. Melt 2 tbsp (30 mL) butter in nonstick skillet. Add oatmeal and cook, stirring, over medium-high heat for 4 minutes or until browned and fragrant. Transfer to slow cooker stoneware and continue with cooking as directed.

STEEL-CUT OATS

Steel-cut (or Irish) oats are more coarsely ground and have a chewier texture than Scottish (or rolled) oats. Scottish oats are ground into a meal, making for a creamier porridge. Rolled oats (also known as large-flake or old-fashioned oats) are steamed first, then rolled, which allows them to cook a little faster. Make sure you don't use quick-cooking rolled oats in this recipe.

BAKED APPLE BREAKFAST COBBLER

SERVES 4 TO 6 | 4- TO 6-QUART SLOW COOKER, STONEWARE GREASED

There's nothing like starting the day with a warm breakfast, except maybe smelling it cooking while you are still in bed. That's the beauty of this slow cooker breakfast cobbler. Prepare all of the ingredients and assemble it right after dinner. Then, before you head to bed, press the Start button. You will love the smell you wake up to!

6 apples, peeled, cored and quartered

1 tbsp (15 mL) freshly squeezed lemon juice

2 tbsp (30 mL) pure maple syrup

1 tsp (5 mL) ground cinnamon

2 cups (500 mL) prepared granola cereal

2 tbsp (30 mL) butter, melted

¼ cup (60 mL) toasted slivered almonds

Vanilla-flavored yogurt

1 Place apples in bottom of prepared slow cooker stoneware. Drizzle with lemon juice and gently toss to coat. Drizzle with maple syrup and sprinkle with cinnamon. Top with granola and drizzle with butter.

2 Cover and cook on Low for 8 hours or until apples are tender and sauce is bubbling.

3 Spoon into serving bowls and top with almonds and a dollop of yogurt.

TIPS

To toast almonds, spread nuts in a single layer in a shallow baking pan or rimmed baking sheet. Bake in a 350°F (180°C) oven, stirring or shaking once or twice, for 5 to 10 minutes or until golden brown and fragrant.

You can use low-fat granola for this recipe.

BAKING APPLES

The best baking apples are those that maintain their shape but become nice and tender and have a sweet-tart flavor that really says "apple" when they're cooked. Some of the best varieties for this dish are Cortland, Golden Delicious, Granny Smith, Braeburn and Jonagold.

GOOD MORNING GRANOLA

MAKES ABOUT 4 CUPS (1 L) | 5- TO 6-QUART SLOW COOKER

This crunchy mix is a perfect topping on hot cereal or yogurt. It also tastes great served on its own with milk.

2 cups (500 mL) large-flake rolled oats

¼ cup (60 mL) raw wheat germ

2 tbsp (30 mL) sesame seeds

½ cup (125 mL) chopped almonds or pecans

½ cup (125 mL) flaked sweetened coconut

½ cup (125 mL) liquid honey

¼ cup (60 mL) frozen cranberry juice cocktail concentrate, thawed

¼ cup (60 mL) butter, melted

2 tbsp (30 mL) packed brown sugar

1½ tsp (7 mL) vanilla

1 cup (250 mL) dried fruit (see tip, below)

½ cup (125 mL) raisins

1 In slow cooker stoneware, combine oats, wheat germ, sesame seeds, almonds and coconut.

2 In a bowl, combine honey, cranberry juice concentrate, melted butter, brown sugar and vanilla. Mix well and pour over oat mixture. Stir to combine.

3 Cook, uncovered, on High for 2 to 3 hours, or until most of liquid has evaporated. Stir every 30 minutes during cooking time.

4 Reduce heat to Low, cover and cook for 3 to 4 hours longer, or until granola is dry and crisp. Stir frequently to prevent over-browning.

5 Spread granola over a foil-lined baking sheet and cool to room temperature. Mix in dried fruit and raisins and store in an airtight container at room temperature for up to 1 month.

TIPS

If your liquid honey has crystallized or if, like me, you use solid creamed honey, place the jar (or as much as you need in a small bowl) in a saucepan of hot water, heating gently until melted. Or heat in microwave until melted.

When measuring honey, rub measuring cup with a little vegetable oil, then measure honey. It will easily pour out, with no sticky mess!

Use dried fruit such as cranberries, cherries or chopped apricots.

VARIATION

You can replace the cranberry cocktail with an equal amount of frozen apple juice concentrate.

NO-BAKE GRANOLA CRUNCHIES

In a double boiler over hot (not boiling) water, melt 1 cup (250 mL) peanut butter, 1 cup (250 mL) milk chocolate chips and ½ cup (125 mL) butter. Stir in 3 cups (750 mL) dry chow mein noodles and 1½ cups (375 mL) granola. Drop by heaping teaspoons onto waxed paper-lined baking sheets. Chill until firm. Store in an airtight container, placing waxed paper between each layer. Refrigerate or freeze for up to 2 weeks. Makes about 4 dozen cookies.

MEXICAN WEEKEND BRUNCH BAKE

SERVES 6 TO 8 | 4- TO 6-QUART SLOW COOKER, STONEWARE GREASED

This is an ideal brunch or light supper idea — sausage and eggs with a Mexican twist. Invite some friends over, pour the mimosas and enjoy a fun meal.

2 lbs (1 kg) hot or mild Italian sausage, casings removed

2 cans (each 4½ oz/128 g) chopped green chilies

4 corn tortillas, cut into 1-inch (2.5 cm) strips

2 cups (500 mL) shredded Monterey Jack or Mexican-style cheese combination

½ cup (125 mL) milk

8 eggs

½ tsp (2 mL) ground cumin

Paprika

1 tomato, thinly sliced

Salsa

Sour cream

1 In a large nonstick skillet, cook sausage over medium-high heat, breaking up with a spoon. Drain well.

2 In prepared slow cooker stoneware, layer half the green chilies, half the tortilla strips, half the sausage and then half the cheese. Repeat the layers.

3 In a bowl, beat together milk, eggs and cumin. Pour over sausage mixture. Sprinkle with paprika. Cover and refrigerate overnight.

4 The next day, set insert in slow cooker. Top with tomato slices. Cover and cook on Low for 7 to 9 hours or on High for 3 to 4 hours. Skim off any accumulated fat. Serve topped with salsa and sour cream.

TIPS

Mild green chilies are found in the Mexican foods section of the supermarket. They are sold whole or chopped.

Look for corn tortillas in the deli department of the supermarket or where flour tortillas are sold. If you have difficulty finding them, substitute tortilla chips. Don't use flour tortillas, since they will become soggy.

SAVORY BRUNCH BREAD PUDDING

SERVES 4 TO 6 | 4- TO 6-QUART SLOW COOKER, STONEWARE GREASED

More commonly known as a "strata," this layered dish makes a great brunch when you have company over, because it can be assembled the night before, then cooked in the morning. When I tested this dish, it earned the comment "Absolutely delicious!" Serve it with a mixed fruit salad.

2 tbsp (30 mL) butter

8 oz (250 g) mushrooms, sliced

1 onion, minced

1 loaf day-old Italian bread, cut into 12 to 16 slices

8 oz (250 g) prosciutto, chopped

2 cups (500 mL) shredded Cheddar or fontina cheese

3 eggs

2½ cups (625 mL) whole milk

1 tbsp (15 mL) chopped fresh parsley

1 In a nonstick skillet, melt butter over medium-high heat. Sauté mushrooms and onions for 5 to 7 minutes or until tender and liquid has evaporated. Set aside.

2 Place half the bread slices in a single layer on the bottom of prepared slow cooker stoneware. Top with prosciutto, cheese and mushroom mixture. Place remaining bread over top.

3 In a blender or food processor, blend eggs and milk until well combined. Pour evenly over mixture in slow cooker.

4 Cover and cook on Low for 3 to 4 hours or until top is golden brown. Sprinkle with parsley before serving.

MAKE AHEAD This dish can be assembled up to 12 hours in advance. Prepare through step 3, cover and refrigerate overnight. The next day, let stoneware stand at room temperature for 10 minutes, then place in slow cooker and proceed with step 4.

TIP

You might think that bread starts to go stale days after it is made, but the process actually begins as soon as the loaf leaves the oven and starts to cool. How quickly it goes stale depends on what ingredients went into it, how it was baked and how it is stored. For this recipe, purchase the loaf a day or two ahead. You can also use ordinary white bread; just cut each slice into quarters.

BANANA WALNUT FRENCH TOAST

SERVES 8 | 5- TO 6-QUART SLOW COOKER, STONEWARE GREASED

Serve this make-ahead French toast with maple syrup as a light lunch or brunch dish.

2 ripe bananas, cut into $\frac{1}{4}$-inch (5 mm) slices

2 tbsp (30 mL) freshly squeezed lemon juice

1 loaf day-old French bread, crust removed, cut into $\frac{1}{2}$-inch (1 cm) cubes (about 10 cups/2.5 L)

3 eggs, lightly beaten

1 can (12 oz/354 mL) evaporated milk

3 tbsp (45 mL) liquid honey

1 tsp (5 mL) vanilla

$\frac{1}{2}$ tsp (2 mL) ground cinnamon

1 cup (250 mL) chopped toasted walnuts (see box, page 177)

1 tsp (5 mL) granulated sugar

1 In a bowl, gently toss bananas with lemon juice.

2 Arrange half the bread cubes in bottom of prepared slow cooker stoneware. Top bread with bananas. Add remaining bread cubes.

3 In a blender or food processor, combine eggs, evaporated milk, honey, vanilla and cinnamon. Slowly pour egg mixture over bread to coat evenly. Press down lightly with the back of a spoon to moisten all bread.

4 Cover and refrigerate for 8 hours or overnight.

5 Sprinkle bread with walnuts and sugar. Cover and cook on Low for 5 to 7 hours or on High for $2\frac{1}{2}$ to $3\frac{1}{2}$ hours, until golden brown and slightly puffed.

MAKE AHEAD Assemble ingredients in slow cooker up to 24 hours before cooking.

TIP

Evaporated milk holds up extremely well in slow cookers and will not curdle. Don't confuse this milk with the sweetened condensed milk used in desserts and candies.

OVERNIGHT BLUEBERRY FRENCH TOAST

SERVES 6 TO 8 | 5- TO 6-QUART SLOW COOKER, STONEWARE GREASED

This unique breakfast dish, filled with the rich flavor of heavenly blueberries, is perfect for any holiday breakfast or brunch. Turn the slow cooker on early in the morning, and by the time the rest of the house is up, you will have a fabulous dish to serve. Be sure to serve it with maple syrup and, for extra decadence, a little whipped cream.

1 cup (250 mL) lightly packed brown sugar

1¼ tsp (6 mL) ground cinnamon

¼ cup (60 mL) butter, melted

12 slices white, whole wheat or whole-grain bread

1½ cups (375 mL) fresh or frozen blueberries

5 eggs, lightly beaten

1½ cups (375 mL) whole milk

1 tsp (5 mL) vanilla extract

½ tsp (2 mL) salt

Maple syrup, whipped cream and fresh blueberries (optional)

1 In a bowl, combine brown sugar, cinnamon and butter, mixing well. Sprinkle one-third of the mixture evenly over bottom of prepared slow cooker stoneware. Cover with 6 bread slices. Sprinkle with another third of the sugar mixture and scatter berries over top. Top with remaining bread slices. Sprinkle with remaining sugar mixture.

2 In a large bowl, beat eggs, milk, vanilla and salt. Pour evenly into slow cooker. Press down lightly on bread slices. Cover and refrigerate overnight.

3 Place stoneware in slow cooker. Cover and cook on Low for 3 to 4 hours or until eggs are set and browned. Serve with maple syrup, a dollop of whipped cream and blueberries, if desired.

TIP

Packages of frozen blueberries are almost a "pantry staple" in our house. We use them in just about everything. I often pick up a few bags when I see them on sale. There is no need to defrost the berries before using them in this recipe.

CLASSIC CORNBREAD

SERVES 8 | 5- TO 6-QUART SLOW COOKER

This is one of my husband's absolute favorites. Serve it as a side dish with chili or stew, or serve thick slices with warm maple syrup for a dessert treat.

1¼ cups (310 mL) all-purpose flour

¾ cup (175 mL) yellow cornmeal

¼ cup (60 mL) granulated sugar

1 tsp (5 mL) baking powder

1 tsp (5 mL) baking soda

1 tsp (5 mL) salt

1 egg, lightly beaten

1 cup (250 mL) buttermilk or sour milk (see tip, below)

¼ cup (60 mL) vegetable oil

1 Turn slow cooker to Low to preheat stoneware.

2 In a large bowl, combine flour, cornmeal, sugar, baking powder, baking soda and salt.

3 In a small bowl, whisk together egg, buttermilk and oil.

4 Make a well in center of dry ingredients and pour in liquid ingredients. Mix together just until moistened.

5 Pour batter into a lightly greased 8-cup (2 L) soufflé dish or 2-lb (1 kg) coffee can and cover with foil. (There is no need to secure the foil with an elastic band or string since there is no water in the bottom of the slow cooker.) Place in bottom of preheated slow cooker stoneware.

6 Cover and cook on Low for 3 to 4 hours or on High for 1½ to 2 hours, until edges of cornbread are golden and a knife inserted in center comes out clean.

TIPS

If you don't have any buttermilk on hand, here is a quick substitution. Place 1 tbsp (15 mL) lemon juice or white vinegar in a glass measuring cup. Add enough milk to make 1 cup (250 mL). Let stand for 5 minutes before using in the recipe.

You may wish to cook the cornbread with the slow cooker lid slightly ajar to allow any condensation to escape.

APPETIZERS, DIPS & DRINKS

ROASTED GARLIC & RED PEPPER HUMMUS

MAKES ABOUT 3 CUPS (750 ML) | 1- TO 3-QUART SLOW COOKER OR SLOW COOKER WARMER

My friends and I love this dip so much that it comes along on our annual Winter Girls' Getaway. It is so simple to cook the chickpeas in the slow cooker, then purée the ingredients in the food processor. Just make sure the chickpeas are very tender before you process them; otherwise, your hummus won't be smooth and creamy. Serve with warm pita wedges, a plate of crudités or whole-grain crackers.

- Preheat oven to 400°F (200°C)
- Food processor

2 cups (500 mL) dried chickpeas, rinsed and drained

6 cups (1.5 L) boiling water

1 head garlic

Olive oil

$\frac{1}{2}$ cup (125 mL) tahini (sesame seed paste)

1 jar (12 oz/340 mL) roasted red peppers, drained (see box, page 35)

$\frac{1}{3}$ cup (75 mL) freshly squeezed lemon juice

Kosher salt

$\frac{1}{4}$ tsp (1 mL) hot pepper sauce, or to taste

Chopped fresh parsley

1 Place chickpeas in slow cooker stoneware and add boiling water.

2 Cover and cook on High for $3\frac{1}{2}$ to 4 hours or until chickpeas are tender but still hold their shape. Drain, reserving $\frac{1}{2}$ cup (125 mL) of the water. Cool to room temperature.

3 Meanwhile, peel away outer skins from garlic head, leaving skins of individual cloves intact. With a sharp knife, cut $\frac{1}{4}$ to $\frac{1}{2}$ inch (0.5 to 1 cm) from the top of the head, exposing individual cloves. Place, base down, on a square of foil or in a garlic baker. Drizzle exposed cloves with oil until well coated; enclose in foil or cover with lid of baker. Bake in preheated oven for 30 to 35 minutes or until cloves feel soft when pressed. Let cool to room temperature, then remove roasted cloves with a cocktail fork or squeeze them out of their skins.

4 In a food processor, combine chickpeas, garlic, tahini, red peppers, lemon juice, salt and hot pepper sauce; purée until smooth. Hummus should be medium-thick. If it's too thick, add some of the reserved cooking water to thin.

5 Transfer hummus to a shallow bowl, drizzle with oil and garnish with parsley.

TIP

When cooking chickpeas, do not add salt to the cooking liquid. It will toughen the chickpeas and they won't absorb water properly during cooking.

RESTAURANT-STYLE SPINACH & ARTICHOKE DIP

MAKES ABOUT 3 CUPS (750 ML) | 4- TO 6-QUART SLOW COOKER

This is one of my favorite appetizers when we have games nights with friends. It tastes just like the dip served in roadhouse-style restaurants. Serve with warm pita triangles, tortilla chips, breadsticks, pretzels or slices of crusty baguette.

2 cloves garlic, minced

2 packages (each 8 oz/250 g) cream cheese, softened

¼ cup (60 mL) mayonnaise

⅓ cup (75 mL) freshly grated Parmesan cheese

1 package (10 oz/300 g) frozen chopped spinach, thawed and squeezed dry

1 can (14 oz/398 mL) artichoke hearts, rinsed, drained and coarsely chopped

⅔ cup (150 mL) shredded Cheddar cheese

1 In a food processor or bowl, combine garlic, cream cheese, mayonnaise and Parmesan. Process until smooth and creamy.

2 Add spinach and artichokes and combine. Spoon mixture into slow cooker stoneware.

3 Cover and cook on Low for 2 to 3 hours or on High for 1½ to 2 hours, until heated through.

4 Sprinkle with Cheddar, cover and cook on High for 15 to 20 minutes longer, or until cheese melts.

TIP

Different brands of artichoke hearts have different flavors, which will affect the taste of this dip (some taste more vinegary than others). Use your favorite brand; you could also use marinated artichokes.

VARIATION

Roasted Red Pepper and Artichoke Dip: Use Asiago cheese in place of Parmesan. Omit spinach and Cheddar. Add 2 chopped roasted red bell peppers (see box, below) with artichokes.

ROASTING RED PEPPERS

For convenience, roasted red peppers are available in jars or can be found fresh in the deli section of some supermarkets. To make your own, preheat broiler and cut red peppers in half, removing pith and seeds. Place cut side down on a baking sheet. Broil until all skin turns black. Place in paper bag and close up. Allow peppers to sweat for approximately 30 minutes. Peel off skins and chop as needed.

CHIPOTLE BLACK BEAN DIP

MAKES 6 CUPS (1.5 L) | 4- TO 6-QUART SLOW COOKER

This is a great party dip that can be assembled up to 2 days ahead. It's perfect for serving at big football get-togethers with friends.

• Food processor

1 tomato, seeded and diced

Coarse salt

2 tbsp (30 mL) olive oil

1 large onion, finely diced

3 cloves garlic, minced

1 tbsp (15 mL) chili powder

4 cups (1 L) cooked or canned black beans (see page 16), drained and rinsed, divided

1 tsp (5 mL) minced chipotle peppers in adobo sauce, plus 1 tbsp (15 mL) adobo sauce

¼ cup (60 mL) water

1 tbsp (15 mL) cider vinegar

1 cup (250 mL) fresh or frozen corn kernels (thawed if frozen)

2 cups (500 mL) shredded Cheddar cheese or Tex-Mex cheese blend, divided

¼ cup (60 mL) chopped fresh cilantro

Freshly ground black pepper

Tortilla chips

1 Place tomato in a colander set in the sink or a bowl and sprinkle with 1 tsp (5 mL) salt. Let stand until juices drain off.

2 In a large skillet, heat oil over medium-high heat. Reduce heat to medium, add onion and sauté for 4 to 6 minutes or until softened and translucent. Add garlic and chili powder; sauté for 1 minute. Add half the black beans, chipotle peppers, adobo sauce and water; bring to a boil. Boil, stirring, for 2 to 3 minutes or until liquid is reduced by half.

3 Transfer bean mixture to a food processor, add vinegar and process until smooth. Let cool for 8 to 10 minutes or until steam subsides, then transfer to slow cooker stoneware. Stir in the remaining beans, tomato, corn, 1 cup (250 mL) of the cheese and cilantro. Season to taste with salt and black pepper.

4 Cover and cook on Low for 3 to 4 hours or on High for 1 to 2 hours, until bubbling. Sprinkle with remaining cheese, cover and cook for 20 minutes or until cheese has melted.

MAKE AHEAD This dip can be assembled up to 2 days in advance. Prepare through step 3, cover and refrigerate. When ready to cook, place stoneware in slow cooker and proceed with step 4.

TIPS

To ripen tomatoes, place them in a brown paper bag and store at room temperature. Never store tomatoes in the refrigerator, as it destroys their delicate flavor.

Once opened, transfer canned chipotle peppers and their sauce to a glass jar with a tight-fitting lid and store in the refrigerator for up to 10 days. For longer storage, transfer the peppers and sauce to a freezer bag and gently press out the air, then seal the bag. Manipulate the bag to separate the peppers, so it will be easy to break off a frozen section of pepper and sauce without thawing the whole package.

Cooking times can vary a great deal between slow cooker manufacturers. Always let your food cook for the minimum amount of time before testing for doneness.

CHIPOTLE PEPPERS

A chipotle pepper is a red jalapeño chile, dried and smoked using a special process. Chipotles have a unique warm heat and smoky flavor, and are often canned in a red adobo sauce made from ground chiles, herbs and vinegar.

RED THAI CURRY WINGS

SERVES 16 AS AN APPETIZER OR 4 AS A MAIN COURSE | 4- TO 6-QUART SLOW COOKER

These chicken wings, coated in a wonderfully sweet and spicy coconut-curry glaze, are especially great for cocktail parties because they're small yet filling.

- Preheat broiler with rack positioned 6 inches (15 cm) from heat
- Rimmed baking sheet, lined with foil

1 small onion, finely chopped

¾ cup (175 mL) unsweetened coconut milk

3 tbsp (45 mL) fish sauce

2 to 3 tbsp (30 to 45 mL) Thai red curry paste

3 lbs (1.5 kg) split chicken wings (see tip, below)

2 tbsp (30 mL) cornstarch

2 tbsp (30 mL) cold water

¼ cup (60 mL) finely chopped fresh cilantro (optional)

1 In a large bowl, combine onion, coconut milk, fish sauce and curry paste; set aside.

2 Arrange chicken wings in a single layer on prepared baking sheet. Broil, turning once, for 15 to 20 minutes or until golden. Transfer wings to slow cooker stoneware. (Discard drippings.) Pour reserved coconut milk mixture over wings and toss gently to coat.

3 Cover and cook on Low for 3 to 4 hours or on High for 1½ to 2 hours, until wings are tender.

4 Using a slotted spoon, transfer chicken to a warmed platter; cover with foil to keep warm. Skim fat from sauce.

5 In a saucepan, combine cornstarch and water. Whisk in sauce and bring to a boil over high heat. Reduce heat and simmer, stirring, for 4 to 6 minutes or until thick and bubbling. Pour into serving bowl.

6 Garnish wings with cilantro (if using). Serve with sauce on the side.

TIPS

Red curry paste is often available in the Asian food section of the supermarket. It is popular in Thai and Indian dishes, and adds a wonderful zing to most recipes. If you can't find it, use curry powder, instead.

Wings are much easier to eat when they are split. If wings are not split when you buy them, remove and discard the wing tips, then cut each wing at joint to make two pieces.

Canned coconut milk is made from grated soaked coconut pulp — it's not the liquid found inside the coconut. It can be found in the Asian food section of the supermarket or in Asian food stores. Be sure you don't buy coconut cream, often used to make tropical drinks such as piña coladas.

SPANISH CHORIZO DIPPERS WITH GARLIC AÏOLI

SERVES 8 | 3- TO 4-QUART SLOW COOKER

This tapas-style appetizer reminds me of my trip to Spain. Enjoy these dippers with a glass of red wine, some cured olives and good Spanish country-style bread.

1½ lbs (750 g) dry-cured chorizo sausage, cut into 1-inch (2.5 cm) thick slices

2 cloves garlic, minced

⅔ cup (150 mL) dry red wine

1 tbsp (15 mL) minced fresh parsley

Country-style bread, sliced

GARLIC AÏOLI

3 cloves garlic

¼ tsp (1 mL) coarse salt

½ cup (125 mL) mayonnaise

2 tbsp (30 mL) olive oil

1 tbsp (15 mL) freshly squeezed lemon juice

1 tsp (5 mL) sweet paprika

Salt and freshly ground black pepper

1 In slow cooker stoneware, combine sausage, garlic and red wine.

2 Cover and cook on Low, stirring once or twice, for 2 to 3 hours.

3 AÏOLI: Meanwhile, with the flat side of a knife, mash garlic and salt until paste forms. (The coarse grains of salt help breakdown the garlic.) Transfer to a bowl and whisk in mayonnaise, oil, lemon juice and paprika. Season to taste with salt and pepper.

4 Serve the sausages with bread and aïoli.

TIPS

Look for domestic cured chorizo sausages in Hispanic markets, gourmet food shops and some well-stocked supermarkets.

When making the garlic paste, be sure to work on a stable cutting board.

HOISIN-GLAZED MEATBALLS

MAKES ABOUT 24 MEATBALLS | 3- TO 4-QUART SLOW COOKER

You won't be able to stop at just a few of these tasty bites. The sauce makes them irresistible.

• Preheat oven to 350°F (180°C)

PORK BITES

1 lb (500 g) lean ground pork

½ cup (125 mL) dry bread crumbs

2 tbsp (30 mL) hoisin sauce

2 cloves garlic, minced

1 green onion, minced

1 egg, lightly beaten

HOISIN GLAZE

¾ cup (175 mL) hoisin sauce

¾ cup (175 mL) red currant jelly

1 tbsp (15 mL) freshly squeezed lemon juice

2 cloves garlic, minced

1 tbsp (15 mL) grated gingerroot (or 1 tsp/5 mL ground ginger)

Sesame seeds

1 PORK BITES: In a bowl, combine pork, bread crumbs, hoisin sauce, garlic, green onion and egg; mix well. Shape into 1-inch (2.5 cm) balls.

2 Arrange meatballs in a single layer on a foil-lined baking sheet and bake in preheated oven for 20 minutes or until browned. Drain off any accumulated juices and transfer to slow cooker stoneware. Discard foil and drippings.

3 HOISIN GLAZE: In a 4-cup (1 L) measure or bowl, combine hoisin sauce, red currant jelly, lemon juice, garlic and ginger; mix well and pour over meatballs. Cover and cook on Low for 5 to 6 hours or on High for 2 to 3 hours.

4 Meatballs can be served directly from the slow cooker or arranged on a serving platter and sprinkled with sesame seeds.

MAKE AHEAD Pork bites can be cooked up to a day ahead and stored in the refrigerator (or frozen for up to 2 months). To freeze, place in a single layer on a baking sheet and place in the freezer. When frozen, transfer to covered containers or resealable freezer bags. Thaw before placing in sauce.

TIP

Hoisin sauce is a thick, reddish brown sauce made from soybeans and used primarily in Chinese dishes. It can be found in the Asian aisle of the supermarket.

PARTY-STYLE MEATBALLS

MAKES ABOUT 30 MEATBALLS | 3- TO 4-QUART SLOW COOKER

People just can't seem to get enough of this slow cooker party classic with its tangy sweet-and-sour sauce.

- Preheat oven to 400°F (200°C)

MEATBALLS

1 lb (500 g) lean ground pork, turkey or chicken

1 egg, lightly beaten

½ cup (125 mL) dry bread crumbs

3 tbsp (45 mL) finely chopped fresh parsley

2 green onions, finely chopped

1 tsp (5 mL) soy sauce

½ tsp (2 mL) salt

¼ tsp (1 mL) freshly ground black pepper

GRAPE CHILI SAUCE

1 cup (250 mL) chili sauce

1 cup (250 mL) grape jelly

1 tsp (5 mL) freshly squeezed lemon juice

2 tbsp (30 mL) packed brown sugar

1 tbsp (15 mL) soy sauce

1 MEATBALLS: In a large bowl, combine pork, egg, bread crumbs, parsley, green onions, soy sauce, salt and pepper. Mix well and shape into 1-inch (2.5 cm) balls.

2 Arrange meatballs in a single layer on a foil-lined baking sheet and bake in preheated oven for 10 to 12 minutes, or until no longer pink inside. Drain off any accumulated juices and transfer to slow cooker stoneware.

3 GRAPE CHILI SAUCE: In a bowl, combine chili sauce, grape jelly, lemon juice, brown sugar and soy sauce; mix well and pour over meatballs.

4 Cover and cook on High for 3 to 4 hours, or until sauce is bubbly and meatballs are hot.

MAKE AHEAD Meatballs can be made ahead and frozen. Bake meatballs, allow to cool and then freeze for up to a month. Before adding to slow cooker, allow meatballs to defrost for about 30 minutes at room temperature.

TIP

If you are short of time, you can make the meatballs ahead or substitute store-bought precooked frozen meatballs. Defrost for about 30 minutes at room temperature before adding them to the slow cooker.

SWEDISH MEATBALLS

MAKES ABOUT 60 MEATBALLS | 4- TO 6-QUART SLOW COOKER

My yoga instructor, Annika (a beautiful Swedish blonde, of course), passed along her grandmother's recipe for these light and delicate meatballs. They are one of the most popular dishes on the buffet table at any party, but they are also delicious served as a main course over wide egg noodles.

- Preheat oven to 400°F (200°C)
- 15- by 10-inch (38 by 25 cm) rimmed baking sheet, lined with foil

MEATBALLS

2 slices white bread

¼ cup (60 mL) beef broth

1 lb (500 g) lean ground beef

1 lb (500 g) lean ground pork

1 large potato, peeled, cooked and mashed

½ cup (125 mL) shredded white Cheddar cheese

¼ cup (60 mL) table (18%) cream

1½ tsp (7 mL) baking powder

1 large onion, grated

1 egg, lightly beaten

SAUCE

½ cup (125 mL) beef broth

½ cup (125 mL) table (18%) cream

¼ cup (60 mL) lingonberry sauce

2 tbsp (30 mL) cornstarch

1 MEATBALLS: Remove crusts from bread and place in a bowl; pour broth evenly over top and let soak until softened. Squeeze out excess broth.

2 In a large bowl, combine soaked bread, beef, pork, mashed potato, cheese, cream, baking powder, onion and egg. Mix well and shape into 1-inch (2.5 cm) balls.

3 Arrange meatballs in a single layer on prepared baking sheet. Bake in preheated oven, turning once, for 10 to 12 minutes or until no longer pink inside. Drain off any accumulated juices and transfer meatballs to slow cooker stoneware.

4 SAUCE: In a large glass measuring cup, whisk together broth, cream, lingonberry sauce and cornstarch; pour over meatballs.

5 Cover and cook on Low for 6 to 8 hours or on High for 3 to 4 hours, until bubbling.

MAKE AHEAD These meatballs can be baked, cooled, transferred to an airtight container and refrigerated for 1 day. To freeze, place meatballs in a single layer on a rimmed baking sheet and freeze until firm. When frozen, transfer to an airtight storage container and freeze for up to 2 months. To assemble dish, place frozen meatballs in slow cooker stoneware, add sauce and cook on Low for 6 to 8 hours or on High for 3 to 4 hours, until bubbling.

TIPS

Soaking the bread in broth first adds a deliciously different texture to these meatballs. They are quite light and airy, not as heavy as meatballs made with dry bread crumbs.

Broth (or stock) is one of the most indispensable pantry staples. Commercial broth cubes and powders are loaded with salt and just don't deliver the flavor of homemade stock or prepared broth. I like to keep 32-oz (1 L) Tetra Paks on hand, especially the sodium-reduced variety.

If you can't find lingonberry sauce, you can use grape jelly, red currant jelly or cranberry sauce.

Resist the urge to lift the lid and taste or smell whatever is inside the slow cooker as it's cooking. Every peek will increase the cooking time by 20 minutes.

LINGONBERRIES

Lingonberries (also known as cowberries or partridge berries) are a member of the cranberry family and are primarily used in Northern Europe to make jams and jellies. They are smaller and less tart than cultivated cranberries. Lingonberry sauce is found in gourmet food shops and in some supermarkets.

BEST BEER NUTS

MAKES ABOUT 2½ CUPS (625 ML) | 4- TO 6-QUART SLOW COOKER

Who would have thought that these favorite stadium nibblers could be made in the slow cooker? You won't believe the rave reviews you will get, and the cleanup is a lot easier than making them in the oven. Of course, drinking a beer with them is a must!

1 cup (250 mL) granulated sugar	**1** In a small bowl, combine sugar and water.
¼ cup (60 mL) water	
2 cups (500 mL) peanuts, preferably unsalted	**2** Place peanuts in slow cooker stoneware. Pour sugar mixture over nuts and toss to coat.

1 In a small bowl, combine sugar and water.

2 Place peanuts in slow cooker stoneware. Pour sugar mixture over nuts and toss to coat.

3 Cover and cook on High, stirring frequently, for 2 to 3 hours, or until sugar mixture is golden brown and peanuts are toasted.

4 Turn out onto a foil-lined baking sheet and set aside to cool.

TIP

Keep these delicious nuts on hand as extra nibbles for parties. They will keep in an airtight container at room temperature for up to a month. They also make a perfect hostess gift packaged in an attractive container with ribbon tied around it.

ROSEMARY ROASTED PECANS

MAKES 2 CUPS (500 ML) | 4- TO 6-QUART SLOW COOKER

These elegant nuts perk up a plate of seasonal snacks. These are excellent to serve on a cheese or charcuterie board.

- Baking sheet, lined with parchment paper

1 tbsp (15 mL) olive oil

1 tsp (5 mL) dried rosemary

½ tsp (2 mL) coarse salt

2 cups (500 mL) pecan halves

1 In slow cooker stoneware, combine oil, rosemary and salt. Add pecans and toss to coat.

2 Cover and cook on High for 1 hour. Uncover and cook, stirring occasionally, for 1 hour or until lightly browned and fragrant.

3 Transfer pecans to prepared baking sheet and let cool. Once cool, store in an airtight container in the refrigerator for up to 6 weeks or in the freezer for up to 3 months.

TIPS

Because of their high fat content, nuts tend to go rancid quickly. They are best stored in an airtight container in a dark, cool, dry place. The freezer is ideal, and doesn't harm the nuts at all.

Along with a good bottle of red wine, these roasted nuts make a great hostess gift!

FRUIT & NUT TRAIL MIX

MAKES ABOUT 6 CUPS (1.5 L) | 3- TO 4-QUART SLOW COOKER

Chunks of caramelized pecan crunch combine with dried apricots and cherries to make an irresistible tote-along snack. You can toss together a batch in no time. Store in a tightly sealed plastic container and it will keep fresh for up to 1 week.

½ cup (125 mL) granulated sugar

2 tbsp (30 mL) melted butter or margarine

1½ tbsp (22 mL) water

½ tsp (2 mL) vanilla

1½ cups (375 mL) pecan halves

1 cup (250 mL) whole almonds

2 tsp (10 mL) finely grated orange zest

1½ cups (375 mL) sesame sticks or pretzel sticks

1 cup (250 mL) dried apricots

1 cup (250 mL) dried cherries or dried cranberries

1 In a small glass measure, combine sugar, butter, water and vanilla. Place pecans and almonds in slow cooker stoneware; pour butter mixture over nuts and toss to coat.

2 Cover and cook on High, stirring frequently, for 2 to 3 hours, or until sugar mixture is golden brown and nuts are toasted. Stir in orange zest; toss to coat and turn out onto foil-lined baking sheet. Set aside to cool.

3 In a large bowl or airtight storage container, combine nut mixture with sesame sticks, apricots and cherries.

VARIATION

For a delicious bridge mix, try adding chocolate-covered cherries or blueberries to the cooked, cooled mixture.

SPICED APPLE CIDER

SERVES 8 TO 10 | 6- TO 8-QUART SLOW COOKER

As this punch heats up, it fills the house with a spicy welcoming scent. For a colorful presentation, serve in a mug with a red cinnamon-candy swizzle stick for stirring.

2 cinnamon sticks

1 tsp (5 mL) whole cloves

1 tsp (5 mL) whole allspice berries

8 cups (2 L) apple cider

½ cup (125 mL) packed brown sugar

1 orange, sliced

3 large baking apples, cored (optional)

1 Place cinnamon sticks, cloves and allspice on a double thickness of cheesecloth. Bring up corners of cloth and tie with an elastic band or kitchen twine to form a bag.

2 In slow cooker stoneware, combine cider and brown sugar, stirring until sugar dissolves. Add spice bag. Place orange slices on top.

3 Cover and cook on Low for 2 to 5 hours, or until hot. Remove spice bag and discard.

4 **OPTIONAL:** For a decorative touch, cut apples in half crosswise and place cut side down in a 13- by 9-inch (3 L) baking dish. Bake in a 350°F (180°C) oven for 25 minutes, or until apple halves are fork-tender. Place apples in punch, floating skin side up.

MULLED RED WINE

SERVES 12 | 6- TO 8-QUART SLOW COOKER

Any time you are feeling a chill, there's nothing better than a warm mug of mulled red wine.

2 bottles (each 25 oz/750 mL) red wine

2 cups (500 mL) orange juice

2 cups (500 mL) pineapple juice

½ cup (125 mL) granulated sugar

1 lemon, sliced

1 orange, sliced

2 cinnamon sticks

4 whole cloves

4 whole allspice berries

1 In slow cooker stoneware, combine wine, orange juice, pineapple juice, sugar, lemon slices and orange slices. Place cinnamon sticks, cloves and allspice on a double thickness of cheesecloth. Bring up corners of cloth and tie with an elastic band or kitchen twine to form a bag. Float in wine mixture.

2 Cover and cook on Low for 4 hours or until hot. Remove spice bag and citrus slices. Leave temperature set on Low. Slow cooker will keep punch at proper serving temperature for up to 4 hours.

TIP

Don't let the citrus peel float in the wine longer than 4 hours or it will impart a bitter taste to the beverage.

ITALIAN WEDDING SOUP 3/10/2023 good

SERVES 6 TO 8 | 5- TO 7-QUART SLOW COOKER

This soup reminds of the one I'm served when I visit my friend Maria's house. Her mother always has a pot of soup on the stove, or if she doesn't, she will quickly make one for you with whatever ingredients she has on hand.

1 lb (500 g) lean ground beef

1 lb (500 g) lean ground pork

1 cup (250 mL) finely grated Parmesan cheese

1 cup (250 mL) fine dry Italian bread crumbs

2 eggs, lightly beaten

1 bunch flat-leaf (Italian) parsley, finely chopped (about 1 cup/250 mL)

½ tsp (2 mL) salt

½ tsp (2 mL) freshly ground black pepper

6 cups (1.5 L) chicken broth

2 cups (500 mL) packed baby spinach, coarsely chopped, or chopped escarole

2 cups (500 mL) cooked small pasta, such as elbows, tubetti, shells or stars

Freshly grated Parmesan cheese (optional)

1 In a large bowl, combine beef, pork, Parmesan, bread crumbs, eggs, parsley, salt and pepper. Using your hands, roll into ¾-inch (2 cm) meatballs. Place meatballs in slow cooker stoneware. Gently pour in broth.

2 Cover and cook on Low for 8 to 9 hours or on High for 4½ to 5 hours, until soup is bubbling and meatballs are cooked through.

3 Stir in spinach. Cover and cook on High for 10 to 15 minutes or until greens are wilted, bright green and tender. Stir in cooked pasta.

4 Ladle into bowls and sprinkle with additional Parmesan, if desired.

TIP

If you don't have homemade chicken stock, use ready-to-use chicken broth. I like to keep 32-oz (1 L) Tetra Paks of broth on hand, especially the sodium-reduced variety. They come in handy when you're making soups and stews. Another option is to use three 10-oz (284 mL) cans of broth and add enough water to make 6 cups (1.5 L). Avoid broth cubes and powders, which tend to be salty.

PARMESAN CHEESE

Authentic Parmesan cheese (Parmigiano-Reggiano) is expensive, but its flavor is certainly worth the price. Well-wrapped in the refrigerator, a block keeps for months, and it goes a long way when you freshly grate it as you need it. Grated versions found on supermarket shelves have a soapy, salty taste that can't compare with freshly grated Parmesan.

GRILLED CHEESE CROUTONS

MAKES ABOUT 20 CROUTONS

These miniature sandwich-like cubes are a fun addition to any creamy soup. Try them on tomato soup too!

¼ cup (60 mL) butter, softened

¼ tsp (1 mL) dried thyme

4 slices sandwich bread

4 oz (125 g) Cheddar cheese, thinly sliced

1 Heat a large skillet over medium-high heat. In a small bowl, combine butter and thyme. Spread butter mixture over one side of each bread slice. Place 2 slices in the pan, buttered side down. Top each with half the cheese, then with a remaining bread slice, buttered side up.

2 Cook, turning once, for 3 to 5 minutes per side or until toasted on both sides. Let cool slightly, then cut into 1-inch (2.5 cm) squares.

CURRIED SPLIT PEA & SWEET POTATO SOUP

SERVES 6 TO 8 | 5- TO 7-QUART SLOW COOKER

There are as many variations on split pea soup as there are cooks, and Curried Split Pea and Sweet Potato Soup is one of my favorites.

1 tsp (5 mL) vegetable oil

1 tsp (5 mL) cumin seeds

1 tsp (5 mL) fennel seeds

1 tsp (5 mL) grated gingerroot

1 tsp (5 mL) finely minced garlic

1 large onion, finely chopped

1 lb (500 g) dried yellow split peas (about 2 cups/500 mL), sorted, rinsed and drained

1 lb (500 g) smoked pork hock

1½ cups (375 mL) coarsely chopped celery

3 carrots, coarsely chopped

2 sweet potatoes, peeled and coarsely chopped

1 tbsp (15 mL) curry powder

1 tbsp (15 mL) dried marjoram, crushed

2 bay leaves

¼ tsp (1 mL) freshly ground black pepper

6 cups (1.5 L) water

1 In a small skillet, heat oil over medium-high heat. Toast cumin and fennel seeds, stirring constantly, for 10 seconds. (Seeds may or may not begin to pop.) Add ginger, garlic and onion; sauté for about 5 minutes or until onions are tender and translucent and spices are fragrant. Transfer to slow cooker stoneware.

2 Stir in peas, pork hock, celery, carrots, sweet potatoes, curry powder, marjoram, bay leaves and pepper. Stir in water.

3 Cover and cook on Low for 9 to 11 hours or on High for 4½ to 5½ hours, until soup is thick and bubbling and peas are tender.

4 Discard bay leaves. Transfer pork hock to a bowl and let cool slightly. When pork hock is cool enough to handle, remove meat from bone. Discard skin and bone. Coarsely chop meat, return to soup and cook on Low for 20 minutes or until heated through.

MAKE AHEAD This dish can be assembled up to 12 hours in advance. Prepare through step 2, cover and refrigerate overnight. The next day, place stoneware in slow cooker and proceed with step 3.

TIPS

For a smoother consistency, you can purée some of the cooked soup after you remove the pork hock. Use an immersion blender right in the slow cooker for ease, and purée until the desired consistency is reached, or transfer $1\frac{1}{2}$ cups (375 mL) to a blender or food processor and process until smooth, then return purée to slow cooker and continue with recipe.

Dried split peas have been mechanically split along the seam so they will cook faster. It's a good idea to sort them before cooking, to remove any tiny stones or discolored pieces. Then place the peas in a colander and rinse under cold running water until the water is no longer foamy.

ROASTED RED PEPPER & TOMATO SOUP

SERVES 4 TO 6 | 4- TO 6-QUART SLOW COOKER

When I walk through our local farmers' market in August and September, I am overcome with an incredible urge to make as many dishes as I can with the bountiful display of lush, ripe tomatoes and red peppers. This is one of my favorites.

4 large red bell peppers

5 large tomatoes, peeled, seeded and chopped or 1 can (28 oz/796 mL) Italian-style stewed tomatoes, with juices (see box, page 54)

1 onion, finely chopped

1 stalk celery, finely chopped

2 fresh basil leaves (or ½ tsp/2 mL dried)

2 cups (500 mL) chicken broth

1 tbsp (15 mL) tomato paste

2 tsp (10 mL) granulated sugar

Juice of ½ lemon

Salt and freshly ground black pepper

Fresh basil

Whipping (35%) cream (optional)

1 Cut peppers in half and remove seeds. Place cut side down on a baking sheet. Broil or grill until skins are blackened and puffed. Remove from oven and place in a paper bag to steam. When cooled, peel off and discard skins; cut pepper into chunks.

2 Transfer peppers to slow cooker stoneware. Add tomatoes, onion, celery, basil, broth and tomato paste.

3 Cover and cook on Low for 4 to 6 hours or on High for 2 to 3 hours.

4 Purée the soup using an immersion blender or transfer soup, in batches, to a blender or food processor and process until smooth.

5 Return mixture to stoneware. Stir in sugar, lemon juice and salt and pepper to taste. Serve hot or refrigerate and serve cold. Garnish with snips of fresh basil. For a richer soup, drizzle 1 to 2 tbsp (15 to 25 mL) whipping cream into soup bowl before serving.

TIPS

In season, red bell peppers are very inexpensive, so I broil or grill extra and keep them in the freezer to have on hand during the winter months.

If you make this soup in the winter, use vine-ripened tomatoes for best flavor. Add an extra tablespoon (15 mL) of tomato paste after the mixture is puréed.

To ripen tomatoes, place in a paper bag and leave on the counter at room temperature. Never store tomatoes in the refrigerator; it dulls their delicate flavor.

An immersion blender is ideal for puréeing the soup right in the slow cooker without having to transfer it to a blender or food processor.

TOMATO PASTE

Tomato paste is made from tomatoes that have been cooked for several hours until the sauce has thickened and has a rich, concentrated flavor and color. Look for tomato paste in squeezable tubes rather than cans. It is especially easy to use when a recipe calls for smaller quantities. The tubes can be found in Italian grocery stores and some supermarkets. Refrigerate after opening.

HARVEST CORN CHOWDER

SERVES 8 TO 10 | 4- TO 6-QUART SLOW COOKER

The slow cooker isn't just for wintertime fare. I love to make this soup when the harvest of fresh corn appears in late July and August.

4 slices bacon, chopped

2 onions, chopped

2 stalks celery, chopped

2 potatoes, chopped

4 cups (1 L) corn kernels, fresh or frozen

4 cups (1 L) chicken broth

1 bay leaf

1 tsp (5 mL) salt

½ tsp (2 mL) freshly ground black pepper

2 tbsp (30 mL) butter or margarine

2 tbsp (30 mL) all-purpose flour

1 can (12 oz/354 mL) evaporated milk or 1½ cups (375 mL) whipping (35%) cream

1 cup (250 mL) shredded Cheddar cheese

Additional shredded Cheddar cheese

Chopped fresh parsley

1 In a large nonstick skillet, over medium heat, cook bacon, onions and celery for 5 minutes, or until onions are translucent. With a slotted spoon, transfer mixture to slow cooker stoneware. Add potatoes, corn, broth, bay leaf, salt and pepper; stir to combine.

2 Cover and cook on Low for 8 to 10 hours or on High for 4 to 6 hours, until vegetables are tender and soup is bubbling. Remove bay leaf and discard.

3 In a saucepan, over medium-high heat, melt butter. Add flour and stir to make a smooth paste. Slowly add milk, whisking constantly to combine. Bring mixture to a boil, whisking constantly until thickened. Remove from heat and stir in cheese until completely melted. Gradually stir milk sauce mixture into slow cooker.

4 Cover and cook on High for 20 to 30 minutes longer. Serve garnished with additional Cheddar cheese and chopped fresh parsley.

MAKE AHEAD This soup can be made up to the point of thickening. Refrigerate for 3 days or freeze up to 3 months. To reheat, thaw first, place soup in slow cooker with ½ cup (125 mL) water, cover and reheat on High for 2 to 3 hours or on Low for 4 to 6 hours. Continue with Step 3 as directed.

TIPS

To use fresh sweet corn in this recipe, remove the husks and stand cobs on end. Use a sharp knife and cut kernels off cobs.

Serve with a hearty multigrain bread or bagels and glasses of ice-cold lemonade.

For a meatless version, omit bacon and add all ingredients to slow cooker. Cook as directed.

EVAPORATED MILK

Evaporated milk holds up extremely well in slow cookers and will not curdle. Don't confuse this milk with the sweetened condensed milk used in desserts and candies.

CHILIS & BEANS

3/3/23 Not

TOUCHDOWN BEER CHILI

SERVES 6 TO 8 | 4- TO 6-QUART SLOW COOKER

Watching football makes people hungry. All the rooting and cheering really stirs up an appetite. Game day is a good time to take advantage of the ease a slow cooker delivers. This simple, hearty chili with nacho chips will keep everyone satisfied, charged up and focused on the game.

- Preheat oven to 350°F (180°C)
- Rimmed baking sheet

1½ lbs (750 g) lean ground beef

4 cloves garlic, finely chopped

1 large sweet onion, finely chopped

1 can (19 oz/540 mL) diced tomatoes, with juices

1 can (4½ oz/127 mL) diced mild green chiles

1 bottle (12 oz/341 mL) dark beer

2 cups (500 mL) cooked or canned red kidney beans (see page 16), drained and rinsed

1 cup (250 mL) frozen corn kernels, thawed

3 tbsp (45 mL) chili powder

2 tbsp (30 mL) liquid honey

1 tbsp (15 mL) hot pepper sauce

1 tsp (5 mL) curry powder

1 bag (8 oz/225 g) multigrain or blue corn tortilla chips

2 cups (500 mL) shredded Cheddar cheese or Monterey Jack cheese

1 can (8 oz/220 mL) sliced jalapeño peppers, drained

Sour cream (optional)

1 In a large nonstick skillet, cook beef, garlic and onion over medium-high heat, breaking up beef with the back of a wooden spoon, until vegetables are tender and beef is no longer pink. Using a slotted spoon, transfer beef to slow cooker stoneware, draining excess fat and liquid from the pan.

2 Stir in tomatoes with juices, chiles, beer, beans, corn, chili powder, honey, hot pepper sauce and curry powder.

3 Cover and cook on Low for 6 to 8 hours or on High for 3 to 4 hours, until bubbling.

4 Meanwhile, spread tortilla chips over baking sheet. Top with cheese and jalapeños. Bake in preheated oven for 10 to 15 minutes or until Cheddar has melted but is not browned. Transfer to a serving bowl.

5 Ladle chili into bowls and top each with a dollop of sour cream (if using). Serve tortilla chips alongside.

MAKE AHEAD This chili can be assembled up to 12 hours in advance. Prepare through step 2, keeping beef mixture and bean mixture separate. Cover each and refrigerate overnight. The next day, combine beef and bean mixtures in slow cooker stoneware, place in slow cooker and proceed with step 3.

TIP

In a pinch, it's not difficult to make your own tortilla chips. Using a pizza cutter, cut 10-inch (25 cm) flour tortillas into 6 or 8 pieces each, depending on the size of chips you want. Lightly brush both sides of each piece with vegetable oil and season lightly with salt and freshly ground black pepper. Bake in a preheated 450°F (230°C) oven, turning once, for 10 to 12 minutes or until golden brown.

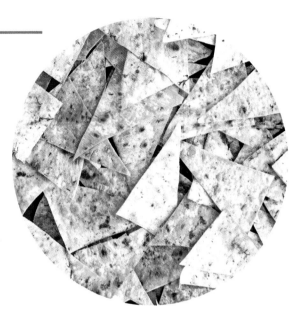

ANTHONY'S AWESOME CHILI

SERVES 6 TO 8 | 5- TO 7-QUART SLOW COOKER

My friend Anthony Scian gave me his "secret" recipe for this very flavorful chili. It's cocoa powder — something Mexican cooks have used for centuries to make their mole sauces.

2 lbs (1 kg) lean ground beef

2 large cloves garlic, minced

2 stalks celery, finely chopped

2 large onions, finely chopped

2 tbsp (30 mL) chili powder

½ tsp (2 mL) dried oregano

¼ tsp (1 mL) cayenne pepper

1 can (28 oz/796 mL) diced tomatoes, with juices

1 can (19 oz/540 mL) red kidney beans, drained and rinsed, or 2 cups (500 mL) home-cooked beans (see page 16)

2 tbsp (30 mL) unsweetened cocoa powder

1 tbsp (15 mL) packed brown sugar

3 or 4 whole cloves

1 tsp (5 mL) white vinegar

½ tsp (2 mL) freshly ground black pepper

1 green bell pepper, finely chopped

Salt and freshly ground black pepper

1 In a large nonstick skillet, over medium heat, cook beef, garlic, celery and onions, breaking up beef with back of a spoon, until vegetables are tender and beef is no longer pink. Add chili powder, oregano and cayenne; cook for 1 minute longer. With a slotted spoon, transfer mixture to slow cooker stoneware.

2 Add tomatoes with juices, kidney beans, cocoa, brown sugar, cloves, vinegar and pepper to slow cooker; stir to combine.

3 Cover and cook on Low for 6 to 8 hours or on High for 3 to 4 hours, until hot and bubbling.

4 Add green pepper and stir to combine. Cover and cook on High for 20 to 25 minutes longer. Season to taste with salt and pepper.

MAKE AHEAD This chili can be assembled 12 hours in advance of cooking (but without adding the green pepper). Follow preparation directions and refrigerate overnight in slow cooker stoneware. The next day, place stoneware in slow cooker and continue cooking as directed.

TIPS

For those who like their chili a little spicier, add more cayenne pepper.

Small quantities of leftover chili should never go to waste. Try spooning this chili over hot baked potatoes. Garnish with grated Cheddar cheese.

CANADIAN MAPLE TURKEY CHILI

SERVES 6 TO 8 | 4- TO 6-QUART SLOW COOKER

Hats off! It's time to make a pot of this chili and sing Canada's national anthem! This chili is slightly sweet, but has lots of meat. It's sure to become a family favorite.

1 tsp (5 mL) vegetable oil

6 slices bacon, chopped

1 onion, finely chopped

1 lb (500 g) lean ground turkey (see tip, opposite)

10 mushrooms, sliced

2 stalks celery, finely chopped

1 large tomato, chopped

½ green bell pepper, finely chopped

½ red bell pepper, finely chopped

1 can (10 oz/284 mL) sodium-reduced condensed tomato soup

1 can (14 oz/398 mL) baked beans in tomato sauce

2 cups (500 mL) home-cooked (see page 16) or canned mixed bean medley (drained and rinsed)

1 cup (250 mL) chopped carrots

2 tbsp (30 mL) pure maple syrup

1 tbsp (15 mL) chili powder

1 tbsp (15 mL) ground cumin

½ tsp (2 mL) salt

½ tsp (2 mL) freshly ground black pepper

⅛ tsp (0.5 mL) cayenne pepper

1 cup (250 mL) frozen corn kernels, thawed

1 In a large skillet, heat oil over medium-high heat. Add bacon and cook, stirring, for 3 to 5 minutes or until slightly crisp. Drain all but 1 tbsp (15 mL) fat from pan. (Discard drained fat.)

2 Add onion and sauté for 3 to 5 minutes or until tender and translucent. Add turkey and cook, breaking up with the back of a wooden spoon, for 5 to 7 minutes or until no longer pink inside. Transfer to slow cooker stoneware.

3 Stir in mushrooms, celery, tomato, green pepper, red pepper, soup, baked beans in tomato sauce, mixed beans, carrots, maple syrup, chili powder, cumin, salt, pepper and cayenne.

4 Cover and cook on Low for 8 to 10 hours or on High for 4 to 5 hours, until bubbling. Stir in corn and cook for 20 minutes.

MAKE AHEAD This dish can be assembled up to 24 hours in advance. Prepare through step 2, keeping turkey mixture and bean mixture separate. Cover each and refrigerate overnight. The next day, combine turkey and bean mixtures in stoneware, place in slow cooker and proceed with step 3.

TIPS

While ground turkey is a wonderful substitute for other ground meats in various popular dishes, it has a much milder flavor than beef or pork. Don't be afraid to increase the seasoning, adding at least twice what you would when using other ground meats.

It's important to fully cook ground meat before adding it to the slow cooker. Cook ground meat until no longer pink inside. Use the back of a wooden spoon to break up the meat as it cooks; otherwise, you will end up with large chunks of meat.

STRATFORD'S SWEET CHILI

SERVES 6 TO 8 | 5- TO 7-QUART SLOW COOKER

My childhood friend Joy Stratford has been a vegetarian for many years. Not only is she a busy mom and great soccer player, she is also a fantastic cook! This is one of her favorite recipes.

1 can (19 oz/540 mL) chickpeas, drained and rinsed, or 2 cups (500 mL) home-cooked chickpeas (see page 16)

1 can (19 oz/540 mL) red kidney beans or black beans, drained and rinsed, or 2 cups (500 mL) home-cooked beans (see page 16)

1 can (28 oz/796 mL) diced tomatoes with herbs and spices

1 can (10 oz/284 mL) corn kernels, drained

2 carrots, peeled and diced

2 large cloves garlic, minced

1 red onion, finely chopped

1 cup (250 mL) ketchup

¼ cup (60 mL) liquid honey

3 tbsp (45 mL) chili powder

½ tsp (2 mL) cayenne pepper

1 green bell pepper, diced

1 red bell pepper, diced

1 yellow bell pepper, diced

Sour cream

Cheddar cheese, shredded

1 In slow cooker stoneware, combine chickpeas, kidney beans, tomatoes, corn, carrots, garlic and red onion.

2 In a bowl, combine ketchup, honey, chili powder and cayenne; mix well and pour into slow cooker. Stir mixture to combine.

3 Cover and cook on Low for 8 to 10 hours or on High for 4 to 6 hours, until hot and bubbling.

4 Add green pepper, red pepper and yellow pepper. Cover and cook on High for 20 to 25 minutes longer.

5 Serve in bowls with a dollop of sour cream and shredded Cheddar cheese.

TIPS

If you find this chili too sweet, reduce the honey by 2 tbsp (25 mL).

Substitute 1 cup (250 mL) frozen corn for canned corn.

Beans are an excellent source of fiber and protein, and give this chili a hearty, filling consistency that satisfies even a die-hard meat eater. Don't be afraid to add an additional can of beans to this recipe. Several varieties of shapes and colors add interest and texture.

WHITE CHICKEN & CORN CHILI

SERVES 4 TO 6 | 4- TO 6-QUART SLOW COOKER

This creamy white chicken and corn chili is so delicious and makes for excellent leftovers (if it's not polished off in one sitting). If you like it a little spicier, add more chili powder and a pinch of cayenne. It's creamy, hearty and full of vibrant spices and flavors.

1 tbsp (15 mL) vegetable oil

2 lbs (1 kg) ground chicken

3 or 4 green onions, finely chopped

2 tsp (10 mL) chili powder

½ tsp (2 mL) dried oregano

Pinch cayenne pepper

2 roasted red bell peppers, diced

2 tbsp (30 mL) pickled jalapeño peppers, finely chopped

3 cloves garlic, minced

1 bay leaf

1 can (19 oz/540 mL) navy beans or white kidney beans, drained and rinsed, or 2 cups (500 mL) home-cooked beans (see page 16)

1½ cups (375 mL) frozen corn kernels

1½ cups (375 mL) chicken broth

½ cup (125 mL) chopped fresh cilantro

2 tbsp (30 mL) freshly squeezed lime juice

1 tbsp (15 mL) granulated sugar

½ tsp (2 mL) salt

Sour cream

1 In a nonstick skillet, heat oil over medium-high heat. Cook chicken and green onions, breaking up meat with back of a spoon, until chicken is no longer pink. Add chili powder, oregano and cayenne; cook for 1 minute longer. With a slotted spoon, transfer mixture to slow cooker stoneware.

2 Add roasted peppers, jalapeño peppers, garlic, bay leaf, beans, corn and broth to slow cooker; stir to combine.

3 Cover and cook on Low for 6 to 8 hours or on High for 3 to 4 hours. Discard bay leaf.

4 Stir in cilantro, lime juice, sugar and salt. Cover and cook on High for 10 minutes longer.

5 Ladle into bowls and garnish with a dollop of sour cream.

MAKE AHEAD Peppers can be broiled or grilled, peeled, then frozen for later use. They will keep up to 3 months in the freezer.

BEST-EVER BAKED BEANS

SERVES 12 TO 15 | 4- TO 6-QUART SLOW COOKER

I like to take this dish to our annual skating party and sleigh ride. When there are a lot of people, it's the perfect pot to pack.

8 oz (250 g) bacon

1 lb (500 g) lean ground beef

2 onions, sliced and separated into rings

2 cans (each 14 oz/398 mL) beans in tomato sauce

1 can (19 oz/540 mL) red kidney beans, drained and rinsed, or 2 cups (500 mL) home-cooked beans (see page 16)

1 can (19 oz/540 mL) chickpeas, drained and rinsed, or 2 cups (500 mL) home-cooked chickpeas (see page 16)

2 cups (500 mL) ketchup

¼ cup (60 mL) granulated sugar

¼ cup (60 mL) packed brown sugar

3 tbsp (45 mL) white vinegar

1 tbsp (15 mL) Dijon mustard

1 In a large nonstick skillet, over medium-high heat, cook bacon for 5 minutes, or until slightly cooked but not crisp. Remove from skillet and place on paper towel–lined plate. Let cool and coarsely chop. Drain excess fat from skillet.

2 Add beef and onions to skillet; cook, breaking up meat with back of a spoon, until meat is no longer pink and onions are translucent. With a slotted spoon, transfer meat mixture to slow cooker stoneware.

3 Add beans in tomato sauce, kidney beans, chickpeas, ketchup, granulated sugar, brown sugar, vinegar, mustard and bacon; stir to combine.

4 Cover and cook on Low for 7 to 9 hours or on High for 3 to 4 hours, until hot and bubbling.

MAKE AHEAD This dish can be assembled in the slow cooker the day before. Refrigerate until ready to cook.

TIP

Serve these beans with garlic bread and a green salad.

BOOZY BAKED BEANS

SERVES 8 TO 10 | 4- TO 6-QUART SLOW COOKER

This recipe was passed along to me by my friend Carolyn Culp. She is always the hit of the family reunion when she turns up with this. You can omit the rum, if you want, but it really adds spirit to this dish.

1 lb (500 g) dried white pea beans (about 2 cups/500 mL), rinsed and sorted

10 cups (2.5 L) water

1 can (14 oz/398 mL) pineapple chunks, with juice

4 oz (125 g) salt pork

½ cup (125 mL) amber or dark rum

¼ cup (60 mL) light (fancy) molasses

¼ cup (60 mL) packed dark brown sugar

2 tsp (10 mL) dry mustard

1 tsp (5 mL) salt

1 In a large saucepan, combine beans and water; bring to a boil over high heat. Reduce heat and simmer for 3 minutes. Remove from heat, cover and let soak for 1 hour. Drain and rinse, reserving 1 cup (250 mL) of the soaking liquid.

2 In slow cooker stoneware, combine reserved soaking liquid, pineapple with juice, salt pork, rum, molasses, brown sugar and mustard. Stir in beans.

3 Cover and cook on Low for 8 hours or until bubbling. Season with salt.

TIP

If using fresh pineapple, substitute 1½ cups (375 mL) fresh pineapple chunks and ½ cup (125 mL) unsweetened apple juice for the pineapple juice.

WHITE PEA BEANS

White pea beans, also known as navy beans or alubias chicas, are the type of cooked bean you will find in canned baked beans in tomato sauce (aka pork and beans). The term "navy bean" was adopted during the Second World War, when pork and beans was regularly fed to the troops.

BEEF

BOLOGNESE SAUCE

SERVES 6 TO 8 | 4- TO 6-QUART SLOW COOKER

My good friend Anthony Scian, a brilliant computer engineer, loves to cook. He will spend Sundays making a big pot of this sauce so his family can enjoy it during the week. Serve it over hot pasta, sprinkled with grated Parmesan cheese.

1 lb (500 g) lean ground beef

½ lb (250 g) lean ground pork or turkey

2 onions, finely chopped

4 cloves garlic, minced

1 stalk celery, finely chopped

1 tbsp (15 mL) dried Italian seasoning (see box, page 105)

1 can (28 oz/796 mL) diced tomatoes, with juices

1 carrot, peeled and finely chopped

1 red bell pepper, finely chopped

8 oz (250 g) mushrooms, sliced

1 can (28 oz/796 mL) pasta sauce

3 whole cloves

1 tbsp (15 mL) balsamic vinegar

2 tbsp (30 mL) butter (optional)

1 In a large nonstick skillet, over medium-high heat, combine beef, pork, onions, garlic, celery and Italian seasoning. Cook, breaking up meat with back of a spoon, until vegetables are tender and meat is no longer pink. Drain and transfer to slow cooker stoneware.

2 Add tomatoes with juices, carrot, red pepper, mushrooms, pasta sauce and cloves to slow cooker. Stir to combine.

3 Cover and cook on Low for 8 to 10 hours or on High for 4 to 6 hours, until hot and bubbling.

4 Stir in vinegar and butter (if using). Cover and cook on High for 5 to 10 minutes longer, or until butter is completely melted.

MAKE AHEAD This dish can be completely assembled up to 24 hours before cooking. Chill ground meat mixture completely before combining with other sauce ingredients. Refrigerate sauce overnight in slow cooker stoneware. The next day, place stoneware in slow cooker and continue to cook as directed.

TIP

Anthony's mother taught him two rules for making pasta sauce: never use tomato paste and always add a little butter and vinegar at the end for a smooth, rich flavor.

CHEESEBURGER SLOPPY JOES

SERVES 4 TO 6 | 4- TO 6-QUART SLOW COOKER

This dish is a great choice for those nights when everyone is coming and going at different times, since you can leave it simmering in the slow cooker and people can help themselves.

2 lbs (1 kg) lean ground beef or turkey

1 onion, finely chopped

2 stalks celery, finely chopped

1 can (10 oz/284 mL) condensed tomato soup, undiluted

¼ cup (60 mL) water

2 tbsp (30 mL) tomato paste

1 tbsp (15 mL) Worcestershire sauce

2 tsp (10 mL) dried Italian seasoning (see box, page 105)

1 cup (250 mL) diced Cheddar cheese (½-inch/1 cm cubes)

Salt and freshly ground black pepper

4 to 6 kaiser buns, split and toasted

1 In a large nonstick skillet, over medium-high heat, cook beef, breaking up with back of a spoon, until no longer pink. With a slotted spoon, transfer meat to slow cooker.

2 Add onion, celery, tomato soup, water, tomato paste, Worcestershire sauce and Italian seasoning to slow cooker; stir to combine.

3 Cover and cook on Low for 6 to 10 hours or on High for 3 to 4 hours, until hot and bubbling.

4 Reduce heat to Low. Add cheese cubes. Cover and cook for 10 to 15 minutes longer, or until cheese melts. Season to taste with salt and pepper.

5 Spoon mixture over half a kaiser bun and top with the other half.

TIP

Serve over toasted kaiser rolls or whole wheat toast and add a tossed green salad for a delicious meal.

CHILI MAC & JACK

SERVES 16 | 6- TO 8-QUART SLOW COOKER

This is traditional mac and cheese with a little sass! Chili improves with age, so some say this dish tastes even better the next day. Semisweet chocolate enriches and enhances the chili. Use the leftovers the next day for your children's lunches. In the morning, warm the chili in the microwave or on the stove, then pop each portion into a Thermos. They will be so pleased!

2 lbs (1 kg) lean ground beef or turkey

2 large onions, chopped

1 jalapeño pepper, seeded and chopped

1 jar (28 oz/796 mL) prepared tomato pasta sauce

2 cups (500 mL) cooked or canned red kidney beans (see page 16), drained and rinsed

2 tbsp (30 mL) chili powder

2 tbsp (30 mL) semisweet chocolate chips

1 tbsp (15 mL) cider vinegar

1 tsp (5 mL) ground cinnamon

¼ tsp (1 mL) ground allspice

Water

2 cups (500 mL) diced Monterey Jack cheese

1 lb (500 g) short pasta, such as ziti, wagon wheels or gemelli

Shredded Monterey Jack cheese (optional)

Chopped onion (optional)

1 In a large nonstick skillet, cook beef and onions over medium-high heat, breaking up beef with the back of a wooden spoon, for 3 to 5 minutes or until beef is no longer pink. Using a slotted spoon, transfer to slow cooker stoneware.

2 Stir in jalapeño, pasta sauce, beans, chili powder, chocolate chips, vinegar, cinnamon, allspice and ½ cup (125 mL) water.

3 Cover and cook on Low for 6 to 8 hours or on High for 3 to 4 hours, until bubbling.

4 In a pot of boiling salted water, cook ziti according to package directions until tender but firm (al dente). Drain.

5 Toss ziti and diced cheese into beef mixture in stoneware. Cover and cook on Low for 10 to 15 minutes or until cheese is melted.

6 Ladle into individual serving bowls. Sprinkle with shredded cheese and onion (if using).

TIP

When handling hot peppers, keep your hands away from your eyes and skin. Better yet, wear rubber gloves and wash your hands and utensils afterwards.

NATIONAL'S CHILI DOGS

SERVES 10 | 5- TO 7-QUART SLOW COOKER

My husband is on a quest to visit every major-league ballpark across the country. When I get to tag along, I look for the ballpark food specialty. At Nationals Park, we were served a Cincinnati-style chili over steamed hot dogs, which was my inspiration for this recipe. Kids love them and they make a great choice for tailgate parties.

CHILI SAUCE

2 lbs (1 kg) lean ground beef

1 large onion, chopped

3 cloves garlic, minced

1 can (14 oz/398 mL) diced tomatoes, with juices

1 can (4½ oz/127 mL) diced mild green chiles

1 tbsp (15 mL) chili powder

1 tsp (5 mL) granulated sugar

1 tsp (5 mL) paprika

½ tsp (2 mL) ground cumin

½ tsp (2 mL) celery seeds

¼ tsp (1 mL) salt

¼ tsp (1 mL) freshly ground black pepper

1 tbsp (15 mL) prepared mustard

1 tsp (5 mL) Worcestershire sauce

20 hot dog wieners (or 10 jumbo-size), warmed

20 hot dog buns (or 10 jumbo-size), split and toasted

Shredded Cheddar cheese (optional)

Chopped onion (optional)

Prepared mustard (optional)

1 CHILI SAUCE: In a large skillet, cook beef, onion and garlic over medium-high heat, breaking up beef with the back of a wooden spoon, for 6 to 8 minutes or until vegetables are tender and beef is no longer pink. Drain off excess fat. Stir in tomatoes with juices, chiles, chili powder, sugar, paprika, cumin, celery seeds, salt, pepper, mustard and Worcestershire sauce.

2 Arrange wieners in slow cooker stoneware. Spoon beef mixture over top.

3 Cover and cook on Low for 4 to 5 hours or on High for 2 to 2½ hours, until bubbling.

4 Using tongs, transfer wieners to buns. Top each with about ⅓ cup (75 mL) sauce and garnish with cheese, onion and mustard (if using).

TIP

Any type of hot dog wiener will work, but slightly firmer all-beef or turkey hot dogs are best.

ITALIAN STUFFED PEPPERS

SERVES 6 | 6- TO 8-QUART SLOW COOKER

Stuffed peppers are a classic slow cooker meal. They are quick and easy to prepare, and this recipe will be a welcome addition to your family's repertoire. It is best to use an oval slow cooker so that the peppers fit in one layer.

6 small to medium red, yellow and/or green bell peppers, tops removed, cored and seeded

1 lb (500 g) lean ground veal

1½ cups (375 mL) cooked rice (about ½ cup/125 mL uncooked)

2 eggs, lightly beaten

2 cloves garlic, minced

⅓ cup (75 mL) freshly grated Parmesan cheese

2 tbsp (30 mL) finely chopped fresh parsley

½ tsp (2 mL) salt

¼ tsp (1 mL) freshly ground black pepper

1 cup (250 mL) tomato sauce or pasta sauce

1 Cut a small hole in the bottom of each pepper.

2 In a bowl, combine veal, rice, eggs, garlic, Parmesan, parsley, salt and pepper. Spoon meat mixture into peppers. Do not pack down.

3 Stand peppers upright in slow cooker stoneware. Spoon tomato sauce evenly over top of each stuffed pepper.

4 Cover and cook on Low for 4 to 5 hours, or until peppers are tender and a meat thermometer inserted into the center of a pepper reads 170°F (77°C).

TIPS

Cutting a hole in the bottom of the peppers allows moisture and steam to penetrate, promoting even cooking.

You can substitute ground turkey or chicken for the veal, but increase the pepper to ½ tsp (2 mL).

TIPS

There are many types of dried mushrooms, including varieties such as shiitake and chanterelles. When they are properly rehydrated, their flavor and texture are as good as fresh. And if the soaking liquid is incorporated into the recipe, it adds even more flavor. Besides hot water, you can try using red wine or beef stock to soak the mushrooms for this stew.

For an extra-peppery flavor, try adding the optional freshly cracked black peppercorns to the flour used for dredging the beef.

Select lean stewing beef or trim the excess fat from the meat before using. (Trimming may take a little extra time, but the result will be worth it.)

CLASSIC HOMESTYLE BEEF STEW

SERVES 6 TO 8 | 4- TO 6-QUART SLOW COOKER

This stew is just like one my mother used to make when my sisters and I were little girls and she was the busy mom-on-the-run.

¼ cup (60 mL) all-purpose flour

1 tsp (5 mL) salt

½ tsp (2 mL) freshly ground black pepper

2 lbs (1 kg) stewing beef, cut into ½-inch (1 cm) cubes

2 tbsp (30 mL) vegetable oil (approx.)

2 cups (500 mL) beef broth, divided

4 carrots, peeled and sliced

4 potatoes, peeled and chopped

2 stalks celery, chopped

1 large onion, diced or 15 to 20 white pearl onions, peeled

1 can (19 oz/540 mL) diced tomatoes, with juices

1 bay leaf

1 tbsp (15 mL) Worcestershire sauce

¼ cup (60 mL) chopped fresh parsley (or 2 tbsp/25 mL dried)

1 cup (250 mL) frozen peas

Salt and freshly ground black pepper

1 In a heavy plastic bag, combine flour, salt and pepper. In batches, add beef to flour mixture and toss to coat.

2 In a large nonstick skillet, heat half the oil over medium-high heat. Cook beef in batches, adding more oil as needed, until browned all over.

With a slotted spoon, transfer beef to slow cooker stoneware.

3 Add 1 cup (250 mL) broth to skillet and stir to scrape up any brown bits. Transfer broth mixture to slow cooker. Add carrots, potatoes, celery, onion, tomatoes with juices, remaining broth, bay leaf, Worcestershire sauce and parsley; mix well to combine.

4 Cover and cook on Low for 8 to 10 hours or on High for 4 to 6 hours, until vegetables are tender and stew is bubbling. Discard bay leaf.

5 Add peas. Cover and cook on High for 15 to 20 minutes longer, or until slightly thickened and peas are heated through. Season to taste with salt and pepper.

MAKE AHEAD This dish can be completely assembled up to 24 hours before cooking (with the exception of beef cubes). Chill browned beef separately before assembling dish. Refrigerate remaining ingredients overnight in slow cooker stoneware. The next day, place stoneware in slow cooker, add browned beef and continue to cook as directed.

TIPS

Serve with thick slices of crusty bread to soak up every last drop of the rich gravy.

Store any leftovers in the refrigerator for up to 3 days or freeze for up to 3 months. For best consistency, add ½ cup (125 mL) water before reheating.

VARIATION

For a slight change of pace, I sometimes make this stew with a can of chunky-style tomatoes with roasted garlic and basil.

STEAK & MUSHROOM PUB PIE

SERVES 2 | 3- TO 4-QUART SLOW COOKER

On a family trip to Wales, my son ordered a pie similar to this in a quaint pub. Jack loved it so much, he polished off the whole thing. I've recreated it for the slow cooker, with great results. Adding a little butter to the sauce gives an extra richness to the filling.

FILLING

2 tbsp (30 mL) all-purpose flour

½ tsp (2 mL) dried thyme

¼ tsp (1 mL) salt

⅛ tsp (0.5 mL) freshly ground black pepper

1 lb (500 g) stewing beef, cut into ½-inch (1 cm) cubes

2 tsp (10 mL) vegetable oil

1 bottle (12 oz/341 mL) dark beer, such as Guinness

1 cup (250 mL) quartered button mushrooms

¾ cup (175 mL) chopped onion

1 tsp (5 mL) Worcestershire sauce

1 tbsp (15 mL) butter

TOPPING

1 cup (250 mL) prepared biscuit mix

⅓ cup (75 mL) milk

2 tbsp (30 mL) shredded Cheddar cheese

¼ tsp (1 mL) dried thyme

1 FILLING: In a bowl, combine flour, thyme, salt and pepper. Add beef and toss to coat with flour mixture.

2 In a large nonstick skillet, heat oil over medium-high heat. Cook beef until browned all over. Using a slotted spoon, transfer to slow cooker stoneware.

3 Add beer to skillet and cook, scraping up any brown bits from pan. Transfer to stoneware. Stir in mushrooms, onion, Worcestershire sauce and butter.

4 Cover and cook on Low for 8 to 10 hours or on High for 4 to 5 hours, until beef is fork-tender.

5 TOPPING: In a bowl, stir together biscuit mix, milk, cheese and thyme until a lumpy dough forms. (Do not overmix.) Drop spoonfuls of dough over stew.

6 Cover and cook on High for 20 to 25 minutes or until a tester inserted in center of topping comes out clean.

TIPS

Serve with boiled new potatoes, just as they would in Wales.

If you prefer a browner crust, you can bake the topping in the oven. Top the cooked stew as directed, then transfer stoneware to a 400°F (200°C) oven and bake for 30 to 35 minutes or until topping is golden brown.

Beer has wonderful tenderizing properties, so it's a great addition to a dish that includes less tender cuts of meat, such as stewing beef. Although dark beers, such as stout and porter, have a strong flavor, they will not overpower the cooked dish. You can substitute lighter or non-alcoholic beer, but the flavor might not be quite as good.

HOMESTYLE POT ROAST

SERVES 6 TO 8 | 3- TO 4-QUART SLOW COOKER

I make this pot roast when I want to be reminded of my childhood and the wonderful aromas that greeted me when I walked in the door. Now my adult children love to make it for the same reason.

¼ cup (60 mL) all-purpose flour

Salt and freshly ground black pepper

1 boneless beef cross rib or rump roast (3 to 4 lbs/1.5 to 2 kg)

1 tbsp (15 mL) vegetable oil

2 onions, quartered

4 carrots, peeled and sliced

4 to 6 potatoes, peeled and quartered

1 cup (250 mL) beef broth

1 can (7½ oz/221 mL) tomato sauce

1 clove garlic, minced

½ tsp (2 mL) dried thyme

1 bay leaf

1 In a bowl, season flour with salt and pepper. Pat meat dry and coat on all sides with seasoned flour.

2 In a large skillet, heat oil over medium-high heat. Add meat and cook, turning with wooden spoons, for 7 to 10 minutes, or until browned on all sides. Transfer meat to slow cooker stoneware.

3 Add onions, carrots, potatoes, broth, tomato sauce, garlic, thyme and bay leaf to slow cooker.

4 Cover and cook on Low for 10 to 12 hours or on High for 6 to 8 hours, until vegetables and meat are tender.

5 Remove roast, onions, carrots and potatoes, cover and set aside. Discard bay leaf. Tip slow cooker and skim off any excess fat from surface of gravy; season with additional salt and pepper. Pour gravy into sauceboat. Slice roast, arrange on a serving platter and surround with vegetables. Serve with gravy.

MAKE AHEAD This dish can be completely assembled up to 12 hours in advance of cooking. Follow preparation directions and refrigerate overnight in the slow cooker stoneware. The next day, place stoneware in slow cooker and continue cooking as directed.

TIP

Slow cooking helps to tenderize less expensive cuts of meat. Pot roast benefits from a longer cooking on Low, but if you're short of time, count on 6 hours of simmering on High to produce fork-tender meat.

CRANBERRY CHIPOTLE POT ROAST

SERVES 2 TO 3 | 3- TO 4-QUART SLOW COOKER

When you're making a pot roast for a small household, either buy a large roast and cut it in half (freeze what you don't need) or look for smaller cuts of beef. The butcher will often cut one for you, if you ask. This recipe was a real hit with my parents' condo neighbors — it got a four-fork rating! Mashed potatoes are a must on the side.

1 boneless beef cross rib, chuck or rump roast (1½ to 2 lbs/750 g to 1 kg)

1 clove garlic, minced

½ tsp (2 mL) dried thyme

Salt and freshly ground black pepper

2 tsp (10 mL) vegetable oil

1 small onion, cut into thin wedges

¾ cup (175 mL) whole berry cranberry sauce

½ to 1 tsp (2 to 5 mL) finely chopped chipotle pepper in adobo sauce

1 Sprinkle beef with garlic, thyme and ⅛ tsp (0.5 mL) each salt and pepper.

2 In a large skillet, heat oil over medium-high heat. Cook beef, turning with two wooden spoons, for 7 to 10 minutes, or until browned all over. Transfer to slow cooker stoneware. Arrange onion around beef.

3 In a bowl, combine cranberry sauce and chipotle pepper. Pour over beef.

4 Cover and cook on Low for 8 to 10 hours or on High for 4 to 5 hours, until beef is fork-tender. Using a slotted spoon, transfer beef and onion to a warmed platter, cover with foil and let stand for 10 minutes.

5 Skim off any fat from cooking liquid. Season to taste with salt and pepper. Pour into a gravy boat. Slice roast across the grain and serve with gravy on the side.

TIP

If the sauce is not thick enough for your liking, here is a quick way to thicken it. Transfer the cooking liquid to a small saucepan and bring it to a boil over medium-high heat. In a small bowl, combine 1 tbsp (15 mL) all-purpose flour and 1 tbsp (15 mL) softened butter; whisk into sauce and cook, stirring, until thickened. Spoon over meat when serving.

ITALIAN BEEF SANDWICHES

SERVES 2 TO 3 | 3- TO 4-QUART SLOW COOKER

Flank steak is an underused cut of meat that works really well in the slow cooker. If you have a hard time finding a small steak, just cut one in half and freeze the rest for another recipe. Once the meat is cooked, it shreds easily with two forks. My friend's mom, Sheila, taste-tested this one for me one night. She cooked some noodles the next night and spooned warmed leftover meat and sauce on top for a second great meal.

1 lb (500 g) flank steak

1 clove garlic, minced

1 tbsp (15 mL) chopped sun-dried tomatoes

½ tsp (2 mL) dried oregano

¼ tsp (1 mL) dried rosemary

Pinch hot pepper flakes

1 can (7½ oz/221 mL) tomato sauce

¼ cup (60 mL) roasted red bell pepper, cut into strips

2 4-inch (10 cm) pieces of baguette (or 2 crusty panini rolls), split and toasted

¼ cup (60 mL) shredded provolone cheese

½ small green bell pepper, cut into thin strips

1 Place steak in slow cooker stoneware. Sprinkle with garlic, sun-dried tomatoes, oregano, rosemary and hot pepper flakes. Pour tomato sauce over top.

2 Cover and cook on Low for 7 to 8 hours or on High for 3½ to 4 hours, until steak is fork-tender. Using a slotted spoon, transfer steak to a cutting board. Using two forks, shred meat. Stir roasted red pepper into shredded steak.

3 Spread steak mixture over bottom halves of bread. Drizzle with cooking liquid and sprinkle with cheese and green pepper. Cover with top halves of bread. Serve the remaining cooking liquid on the side, for dipping.

TIPS

Look for reduced-sodium tomato sauce.

To shred meat, hold a fork in each hand and insert the tines, back to back and straight down, into the meat. Gently pull the forks apart, shredding the meat into long, thin strands.

STEAK FAJITAS WITH TOMATO CORN RELISH

SERVES 6 | 4- TO 6-QUART SLOW COOKER

This is a good meal for a casual get-together with friends. Have everything ready and let your guests assemble the fajitas themselves. Make it a Mexican party and throw together some lime margaritas!

1 beef flank steak (about 2 lbs/1 kg), trimmed

2 onions, thinly sliced

2 cloves garlic, finely chopped

1 cup (250 mL) thick and chunky salsa

1½ tsp (7 mL) smoked paprika

1 tsp (5 mL) salt, divided

½ tsp (2 mL) ground cumin

1 red bell pepper, cut into strips

1 yellow bell pepper, cut into strips

12 10-inch (25 cm) cheese-flavored flour tortillas

½ cup (125 mL) sour cream

2 cups (500 mL) shredded Monterey Jack cheese

1 large tomato, diced

1 can (14 oz/398 mL) corn kernels, drained

3 tbsp (45 mL) finely chopped fresh cilantro

1 tbsp (15 mL) freshly squeezed lime juice

¼ tsp (1 mL) freshly ground black pepper

1 Place steak in slow cooker stoneware. Spread onions on top.

2 In a bowl, combine garlic, salsa, paprika, ½ tsp (2 mL) of the salt and cumin. Pour over steak and onions.

3 Cover and cook on Low for 6 to 8 hours or on High for 3 to 4 hours, until steak is tender. Transfer steak to a cutting board or bowl and, using two forks, shred meat. Return to stoneware.

4 Stir in red and yellow bell peppers. Cover and cook on High for 30 to 45 minutes or until peppers are tender-crisp.

5 Meanwhile, in a bowl, combine tomato, corn, cilantro, lime juice and the remaining salt and pepper. Let stand at room temperature for 20 to 30 minutes before serving.

6 Just before serving, preheat oven to 350°F (180°C). Wrap a stack of tortillas in foil and heat in oven for 10 minutes.

7 Spoon about ½ cup (125 mL) of the steak mixture along the center of each tortilla. Top with relish, sour cream and cheese. Fold tortilla around filling (see tip, opposite).

TIPS

If you like heat, add a minced jalapeño to the relish.

How to fill and fold tortillas: Spoon filling along the center of the warm tortilla. Fold the right side of the tortilla over the filling, then fold up the bottom. Fold the left side over the filling and wrap it around to form a tight roll. To prevent drips, wrap a small piece of foil, waxed paper or parchment paper around the bottom of the fajita.

POULTRY

SMOKY CHICKEN CHIPOTLE SOFT TACOS

SERVES 14 TO 16 | 4- TO 6-QUART SLOW COOKER

These perfect party tacos make a great excuse to gather friends and family for a Friday night appetizer. I love the rich, smoky flavor the peppers add to the chicken. Serving the tacos with guacamole and sour cream helps combat the heat of the peppers. Leftovers can be served over nachos or as a topping for baked potatoes or cooked pasta.

5 lbs (2.5 kg) boneless skinless chicken thighs

2 onions, chopped

2 chipotle peppers in adobo sauce, minced, with 1 tbsp (15 mL) sauce

1 Cubanelle pepper, seeded and finely chopped

1 can (5½ oz/156 mL) tomato paste

¾ cup (175 mL) chili sauce

2 tbsp (30 mL) unsweetened cocoa powder

1 tsp (5 mL) ground cumin

¾ tsp (4 mL) salt

½ tsp (2 mL) ground cinnamon

Pinch ground nutmeg

Pinch ground coriander

14 to 16 6- or 7-inch (15 or 18 cm) flour tortillas, warmed (see tip, opposite)

TOPPINGS

Shredded Cheddar cheese or Tex-Mex cheese blend

Diced tomatoes

Diced onions

Sour cream

Guacamole

Shredded lettuce

Salsa

Lime wedges

1 Place chicken in slow cooker stoneware. Stir in onions, chipotle peppers with sauce, Cubanelle pepper, tomato paste, chili sauce, cocoa powder, cumin, salt, cinnamon, nutmeg and coriander.

2 Cover and cook on Low for 6 to 7 hours or until juices run clear when chicken is pierced with a fork.

3 Using two forks, shred chicken in stoneware. Stir with sauce to combine. (Chicken mixture will hold on Low or Warm heat for up to 2 hours; stir occasionally.)

4 Spoon ⅓ cup (75 mL) of the chicken mixture along the center of each tortilla. Sprinkle with desired toppings, squeeze lime juice over top, if desired, and roll up.

Tandoori and tikka curry pastes are complex blends of freshly ground spices and herbs, preserved in vegetable oil to seal in freshness. Both are mild blends and can be mixed with broth, yogurt or canned tomatoes to create a delicious sauce for meat, poultry, seafood or vegetables. Once opened, curry paste can be stored in the refrigerator for up to 6 months.

CHICKEN STEW WITH ROSEMARY DUMPLINGS

SERVES 4 TO 6 | 4- TO 6-QUART SLOW COOKER

Here's the ultimate comfort food — perfect for the entire family to enjoy while gathered at the kitchen table.

½ cup (125 mL) all-purpose flour

1 tsp (5 mL) salt

½ tsp (2 mL) freshly ground black pepper

1 whole chicken (about 3 lbs/1.5 kg), cut into pieces

1 tbsp (15 mL) vegetable oil

4 large carrots, peeled and sliced 1 inch (2.5 cm) thick

2 stalks celery, sliced ½ inch (1 cm) thick

1 onion, thinly sliced

1 tsp (5 mL) dried rosemary

2 cups (500 mL) chicken broth, divided

1 cup (250 mL) frozen peas

DUMPLINGS

1 cup (250 mL) all-purpose flour

2 tsp (10 mL) baking powder

½ tsp (2 mL) dried rosemary

½ tsp (2 mL) salt

½ cup (125 mL) milk

1 egg, lightly beaten

Fresh rosemary sprigs

1 In a heavy plastic bag, combine flour, salt and pepper. In batches, add chicken pieces to flour mixture and toss to coat.

2 In a large nonstick skillet, heat oil over medium-high heat. Add chicken pieces and cook for 8 to 10 minutes, or until brown on all sides. Set aside.

3 Add carrots, celery, onion and rosemary to slow cooker stoneware. Set chicken pieces over vegetables.

4 Pour ½ cup (125 mL) broth into skillet and cook over medium-high heat, scraping up brown bits from bottom of pan. Pour pan juices into slow cooker along with remaining broth.

5 Cover and cook on Low for 8 to 10 hours or on High for 4 to 6 hours, until vegetables are tender and stew is bubbling. Add peas and stir gently to combine.

6 DUMPLINGS: In a bowl, sift together flour, baking powder, rosemary and salt. In a measuring cup, combine milk and egg. Mix well and add to flour mixture. Stir with a fork to make a lumpy dough (do not overmix — lumps are fine). Drop dumpling mixture over chicken pieces. Cover and cook on High for 25 to 30 minutes, or until tester inserted in center of dumpling comes out clean. Serve garnished with fresh rosemary sprigs.

TIPS

This all-in-one meal works especially well in a large slow cooker since it provides plenty of room for the dumplings to cook.

To save some time, make the dumplings with 2 cups (500 mL) prepared biscuit mix combined with $\frac{1}{2}$ tsp (2 mL) crumbled dried rosemary. Add in $\frac{3}{4}$ cup (175 mL) milk and stir until lumpy. Continue with recipe as directed.

For fluffier dumplings, drop the dough on the chicken pieces rather than into the liquid. This will ensure that the dumplings are steamed and don't become soggy from the liquid. Also, for proper steaming, be sure the stew is piping hot.

Cooking times for poultry may be longer for larger slow cookers and/or where there is a relatively high proportion of dark to white meat. For predominantly white-meat dishes, be sure to avoid overcooking.

COCONUT CURRY CHICKEN

SERVES 6 | 4- TO 6-QUART SLOW COOKER

This spicy, fragrant stew is traditionally served over steamed rice. Try basmati or jasmine rice for a more authentic taste sensation.

½ cup (125 mL) all-purpose flour

½ tsp (2 mL) salt

½ tsp (2 mL) freshly ground black pepper

12 skinless chicken thighs

1 tbsp (15 mL) vegetable oil

2 onions, chopped

4 cloves garlic, minced

1 tbsp (15 mL) curry powder (or 2 tbsp/ 30 mL mild curry paste)

½ cup (125 mL) chicken broth

1 can (14 oz/398 mL) coconut milk

4 carrots, peeled and sliced

1 can (19 oz/540 mL) chickpeas, drained and rinsed, or 2 cups (500 mL) home-cooked chickpeas (see page 16)

1 cup (250 mL) fresh or frozen green peas or snow peas (thawed if frozen)

1 Granny Smith apple, unpeeled, cut into 1-inch (2.5 cm) chunks

1 cup (250 mL) plain yogurt

½ cup (125 mL) cashews

¼ cup (60 mL) shredded sweetened coconut, toasted

1 In a heavy plastic bag, combine flour, salt and pepper. In batches, add chicken thighs to flour mixture and toss to coat. Place chicken in slow cooker stoneware, reserving excess flour.

2 In a large nonstick skillet, heat oil over medium-high heat. Add onions, garlic and curry powder. Cook, stirring, for 3 minutes, or until onions are translucent and fragrant. Sprinkle with reserved seasoned flour and cook, stirring, for 1 minute.

3 Stir in broth and coconut milk and bring to a boil. Add carrots and chickpeas. Mix well and pour over chicken in slow cooker.

4 Cover and cook on Low for 5 to 7 hours or on High for 2½ to 4 hours, until juices run clear when chicken is pierced with a fork, vegetables are tender and curry is bubbling.

5 Stir in green peas, apple and yogurt. Cover and cook on High for 15 to 20 minutes longer, or until warmed through. Serve garnished with cashews and coconut.

TOASTING COCONUT

Spread flaked or shredded coconut on a baking sheet. Toast at 300°F (150°C) for 10 to 12 minutes, or until golden.

TIPS

Purchase chicken thighs in economical family packs. Divide into meal-sized portions, wrap in plastic wrap and freeze in freezer bags.

Chopped garlic in the jar is a convenient alternative to fresh garlic. It's easy to use and will keep in the refrigerator for up to 6 months.

Canned coconut milk is made from grated and soaked coconut pulp — not, as you might think, from the liquid found inside the coconut. It can be found in the Asian foods section of most supermarkets or Asian food stores. Be sure you don't buy coconut cream, which is often used for making tropical drinks such as piña coladas.

Cooking times for poultry may be longer for larger slow cookers and/or where there is a relatively high proportion of dark to white meat. For predominantly white-meat dishes, be sure to avoid overcooking.

DRUNKEN ROAST CHICKEN

SERVES 6 TO 8 | 4- TO 6-QUART SLOW COOKER

While roasting is something we typically associate with the oven, you can also "roast" in a slow cooker — with very tasty results. In this recipe, the garlic creates a wonderful aroma and imparts a subtle flavor to the chicken.

1 roasting chicken (about 3½ to 4 lbs/1.75 to 2 kg)

4 to 6 cloves garlic, halved

1 onion, quartered

1 stalk celery, with leaves, cut into 3 pieces

1 tsp (5 mL) dried thyme

½ tsp (2 mL) paprika

½ cup (125 mL) chicken broth

½ cup (125 mL) dry white wine

1 tbsp (15 mL) Worcestershire sauce

GRAVY

1 tbsp (15 mL) butter

1 tbsp (15 mL) all-purpose flour

Salt and freshly ground black pepper

1 Rinse chicken inside and out and pat dry with paper towels. With your fingers, gently loosen skin from chicken breast to form a pocket. Insert garlic halves under the skin. Place onion and celery in the cavity.

2 With kitchen twine, tie chicken legs together and secure wings to body, leaving an extra length of twine at each end. You will use the ends to lift the chicken from slow cooker.

3 Place chicken in slow cooker stoneware, breast side up. Sprinkle with thyme and paprika. Pour in broth, wine and Worcestershire sauce.

4 Cover and cook on Low for 8 to 10 hours, or until a meat thermometer inserted in thigh reads 170°F (77°C).

5 Gently remove chicken from slow cooker and transfer to a platter. Cover with foil to keep warm. If desired, brown chicken under preheated broiler for 5 to 7 minutes.

6 **GRAVY:** Pour 1 cup (250 mL) juices from slow cooker into a glass measure; skim any fat from surface. In a saucepan, melt butter over medium-high heat. Add flour and cook, stirring, for 1 minute. Add measured juices and bring mixture to a boil; cook, stirring, until sauce is smooth and thickened. Season to taste with salt and pepper. Serve gravy over chicken.

TIPS

If you have thyme growing in your herb garden, substitute a few fresh sprigs for the dried thyme called for in this recipe.

If whole chicken is too large to fit in your slow cooker, cut it into pieces with a sharp knife.

Cooking times for poultry may be longer for larger slow cookers and/or where there is a relatively high proportion of dark to white meat. For predominantly white-meat dishes, be sure to avoid overcooking.

MOROCCAN CHICKEN

SERVES 4 TO 6 | 4- TO 6-QUART SLOW COOKER

I love Middle Eastern cuisine. While you're cooking this exotic dish, the pungent aromas of curry and lemon will emanate throughout the house.

½ cup (125 mL) all-purpose flour

1 tbsp (15 mL) garam masala or curry powder

1 tsp (5 mL) salt

½ tsp (2 mL) freshly ground black pepper

3 lbs (1.5 kg) bone-in chicken pieces (skin-on breasts, skinless drumsticks and/or thighs)

2 tbsp (30 mL) olive oil (approx.)

2 onions, chopped

2 cloves garlic, minced

½ cup (125 mL) dry white wine

½ cup (125 mL) chicken broth

Finely grated zest and freshly squeezed juice of 1 lemon

1 preserved lemon (see tip, opposite), finely chopped

½ cup (125 mL) pitted ripe kalamata olives

¼ cup (60 mL) chopped fresh cilantro

1 In a heavy plastic bag, combine flour, garam masala, salt and pepper. In batches, add chicken to bag and toss to coat with flour mixture. (Once all the chicken is coated, reserve the remaining flour mixture.)

2 In a large skillet, heat half the oil over medium-high heat. Cook chicken in batches, adding more oil as needed, for 2 to 3 minutes per side or until browned all over. Using a slotted spoon, transfer to slow cooker stoneware.

3 Add onions to skillet, reduce heat to medium and sauté for about 2 minutes or until tender and translucent. Add garlic and reserved flour mixture; cook, stirring, for about 3 minutes or until flour is toasted. Add wine and broth; cook, stirring, until thickened. Remove from heat and stir in ½ tsp (2 mL) of the lemon zest. Pour over chicken. Scatter preserved lemon on top.

4 Cover and cook on Low for 5 to 6 hours or on High for 2½ to 3 hours, until breasts are no longer pink inside and/or juices run clear when drumsticks and thighs are pierced.

5 Using a slotted spoon, transfer chicken to a platter. Stir remaining lemon zest, lemon juice, olives and cilantro into sauce. Spoon over chicken.

TIP

If using a combination of chicken breasts, drumsticks and thighs, place the breasts on top to prevent them from getting overcooked.

SWEET THAI CHILI CHICKEN

SERVES 5 TO 6 | 4- TO 6-QUART SLOW COOKER

This Thai chicken dish is so good that everyone will want seconds. It blends all of the great flavor profiles found in Thai cooking — sweet, salty, spicy and sour. Serve over hot cooked rice noodles, with Ginger Snow Peas and Peppers (see recipe, below) on the side.

10 to 12 boneless skinless chicken thighs

2 cloves garlic, minced

2 tsp (10 mL) paprika

¼ tsp (1 mL) Chinese five-spice powder

½ cup (125 mL) sweet Thai chili sauce

¼ cup (60 mL) ketchup

2 tbsp (30 mL) fish sauce

2 tbsp (30 mL) water

1 Place chicken thighs in slow cooker stoneware. In a bowl, combine garlic, paprika, five-spice powder, chili sauce, ketchup, fish sauce and water. Pour evenly over chicken.

2 Cover and cook on Low for 5 to 6 hours or on High for $2\frac{1}{2}$ to 3 hours, until juices run clear when chicken is pierced.

CHINESE FIVE SPICE POWDER

If you want to make your own Chinese five-spice powder, you'll need equal amounts of ground cinnamon, cloves, star anise, fennel seeds and Szechuan peppercorns. (You can substitute freshly ground black pepper for the Szechuan peppercorns.) Use a clean coffee grinder or a mortar and pestle to finely grind the spices together.

SQUASH-TOPPED SHEPHERD'S PIE

SERVES 6 | 4- TO 6-QUART SLOW COOKER

Here's a different kind of shepherd's pie — ground chicken and vegetables topped with a buttery yellow squash topping.

1 tbsp (15 mL) vegetable oil

2 lbs (1 kg) lean ground chicken

2 onions, finely chopped

2 cloves garlic, minced

1 carrot, peeled and grated

1 cup (250 mL) frozen corn kernels

⅔ cup (150 mL) tomato paste

¾ cup (175 mL) water

2 tbsp (30 mL) dried parsley (or ¼ cup/60 mL fresh)

2 tsp (10 mL) Worcestershire sauce

1 tsp (5 mL) dried thyme

1 tsp (5 mL) paprika

1 tsp (5 mL) salt

½ tsp (2 mL) freshly ground black pepper

4 cups (1 L) puréed Hubbard squash (see box, opposite)

1 In a large nonstick skillet, heat oil over medium heat. Add ground chicken and cook, breaking up with a spoon, until no longer pink.

2 Add onions, garlic, carrot and corn; cook for 5 minutes, or until vegetables are tender. Stir in tomato paste, water, parsley, Worcestershire sauce, thyme, paprika, salt and pepper, mixing well. Transfer mixture to slow cooker stoneware and cover with squash purée.

3 Cover and cook on Low for 6 to 8 hours or on High for 3 to 4 hours, until bubbling and heated through.

MAKE AHEAD This pie can be assembled the night before. Follow preparation directions and refrigerate overnight in slow cooker stoneware. The next day, place stoneware in slow cooker and continue cooking as directed.

TIPS

Always make sure ground meat is fully cooked before adding it to the slow cooker. Cold uncooked ground meat takes too long to come to a safe temperature. (Cooking and draining the meat first also helps eliminate extra fat and the liquid that accumulates during cooking.)

Once the fall harvest season rolls around, there are many winter squash varieties to choose from. Choose squash that are heavy for their size.

TO MAKE SQUASH PURÉE

Halve a 3-lb (1.5 kg) Hubbard, acorn or butternut squash, then scoop out seeds and pith. Place flesh side down on microwave-safe plate and cover with plastic wrap. Microwave on High for 8 to 12 minutes, or until tender. Or place in a roasting pan, flesh side up. Pour in enough water to come 1 inch (2.5 cm) up sides of pan. Bake in a 400°F (200°C) oven for 30 to 60 minutes. Let cool. Scoop out flesh and purée in a food processor or mash well with a potato masher. Add 1 tbsp (15 mL) packed brown sugar and 2 tbsp (25 mL) butter or margarine to purée, mixing well.

PORK & LAMB

PORK CHILI RIBS

SERVES 2 | 3- TO 4-QUART SLOW COOKER

There's no need to fire up the grill for these ribs — they simmer away on their own in a spunky barbecue sauce. Serve with a side of potato salad for an authentic taste of summer. Shred any leftover meat to fill grilled paninis the next day.

1½ lbs (750 g) pork back ribs, trimmed

1 small onion, finely chopped

1 clove garlic, minced

2 tbsp (30 mL) packed brown sugar

½ tsp (2 mL) chili powder

¼ tsp (1 mL) smoked paprika

¼ tsp (1 mL) celery seeds

½ cup (125 mL) ketchup

½ tsp (2 mL) Worcestershire sauce

¼ tsp (1 mL) hot pepper sauce

½ cup (125 mL) water

1 Place ribs in slow cooker stoneware. In a small bowl, combine onion, garlic, brown sugar, chili powder, paprika, celery seeds, ketchup, Worcestershire sauce, hot pepper sauce and water. Pour over ribs.

2 Cover and cook on Low for 10 to 12 hours or on High for 5 to 6 hours, until ribs are tender. Using a slotted spoon, transfer ribs to a serving platter and keep warm.

3 Skim off any fat from cooking liquid in stoneware. Transfer cooking liquid to a saucepan and bring to a boil. Reduce heat slightly and boil gently for 5 to 7 minutes or until thickened. Serve sauce on the side.

TIP

Here's a foolproof way to chop an onion: Peel the onion and halve it from top to base. Place each half cut side down on a cutting board. Slice horizontally across each half. Holding the slices together, slice vertically.

SMOKED PAPRIKA

Smoked paprika is made by grinding peppers that have undergone a smoking process. You can find it in various heat levels (from mild to hot). Be careful how much you use, because smoky seasonings can easily overpower the flavor of a dish.

SLOW COOKER TO GRILL STICKY RIBS

SERVES 4 | 4- TO 6-QUART SLOW COOKER

This is a great way to use your slow cooker in the hot summer months, without heating up the kitchen.

4 lbs (2 kg) pork back ribs, trimmed of excess fat, cut into serving-sized portions

1 onion, sliced

1 stalk celery, with leaves

2 cloves garlic, peeled and crushed

2 bay leaves

1 tsp (5 mL) whole black peppercorns

STICKY SAUCE

½ cup (125 mL) barbecue sauce

½ cup (125 mL) grape jelly

2 cloves garlic, minced

Dash hot pepper sauce

1 Place ribs in slow cooker stoneware. (For smaller slow cookers, ribs may have to be cut into smaller portions to fit.)

2 Place onion, celery, garlic, bay leaves and peppercorns around ribs. Cover with water.

3 Cover and cook on Low for 6 to 8 hours, or until ribs are tender. Transfer ribs to a bowl. Discard cooking liquid and vegetables.

4 **STICKY SAUCE:** In a saucepan over medium heat, combine barbecue sauce, grape jelly, minced garlic and hot pepper sauce. Cook for 5 minutes, stirring constantly, until jelly has melted.

5 Preheat barbecue and carefully oil grill rack. Brush ribs generously with sauce. Grill ribs over low heat 4 to 6 inches (10 to 15 cm) from coals. Grill for 15 to 20 minutes, or until browned, turning occasionally and brushing with sauce. Discard any remaining sauce.

MAKE AHEAD Prepare these succulent ribs the night before and let them cook in the slow cooker while you are sleeping. Refrigerate the ribs the next morning in the sticky sauce. They will be ready to throw on the grill at the end of the day.

JERK PORK RIBS WITH SWEET POTATOES & MANGO SALAD

SERVES 6 | 4- TO 6-QUART SLOW COOKER

Jerk seasoning, a fiery spice blend, comes to us from the island of Jamaica. While some purist "jerks" may crave the heat, it is actually the flavor notes of thyme and allspice you want to capture in this dish. Serve it with Mango Salad (see recipe, opposite) — the colors are beautiful.

- Preheat broiler, with rack set 6 inches (15 cm) below heat source
- Broiler pan or rimmed baking sheet, lined with foil

3 lbs (1.5 kg) country-style pork ribs, cut into individual ribs, if possible

1 tsp (5 mL) salt

½ tsp (2 mL) freshly ground black pepper

2 tbsp (30 mL) Jamaican jerk seasoning

¼ cup (60 mL) dark rum

2 tbsp (30 mL) vegetable oil

2 tbsp (30 mL) butter, softened

2 lbs (1 kg) sweet potatoes, peeled and cut into ½-inch (1 cm) slices

1 onion, sliced

2 tbsp (30 mL) packed brown sugar

3 green onions, sliced

1 tomato, finely chopped

Mango Salad (see recipe, opposite)

1 Place ribs on prepared broiler pan and season with salt and pepper. Broil, turning once, for 10 to 15 minutes or until browned. Transfer to a plate lined with paper towels and let drain.

2 In a bowl, combine jerk seasoning, rum and oil. Set aside.

3 Spread butter over bottom of slow cooker stoneware. Arrange potatoes and onion on top. Sprinkle with brown sugar. Place ribs on top. Spoon jerk mixture over ribs.

4 Cover and cook on Low for 6 to 8 hours or on High for 3 to 4 hours, until ribs are tender. Using a slotted spoon, transfer potatoes and ribs to a warmed platter and tent with foil to keep warm.

5 Skim fat from cooking liquid, then stir in green onions and tomato. Spoon over ribs. Serve with mango salad alongside.

TIPS

I used a dry jerk rub for this recipe, but a liquid seasoning would work well too.

Country-style ribs are the meatiest cut of pork ribs, but side ribs or spareribs will also work in this recipe. To help reduce the fat in the finished dish, cut the slab into five- or six-rib portions, place in a large pot of water and bring to a boil, then reduce heat and simmer for 30 to 45 minutes. Continue with step 1 as directed.

JERK SEASONING

Originating in Jamaica, jerk seasoning is used to season meat for grilling. The ingredients vary from cook to cook, but it is generally a combination of hot chile peppers and allspice, with additional seasonings such as cinnamon, cloves, thyme, garlic and onions.

MANGO SALAD

SERVES 6

This crisp, colorful salad provides a refreshing contrast to the jerk flavors from the pork ribs. Together, they make a great entertaining menu, as you can start the ribs earlier in the day and toss the salad together at the end. For an extra-peppery flavor, use baby arugula or watercress in place of the Boston lettuce in the salad.

3 green onions, thinly sliced

2 ripe mangos, peeled and cubed

1 head Boston lettuce, leaves separated and torn

1 red bell pepper, thinly sliced

1 cup (250 mL) shredded red cabbage

¼ cup (60 mL) chopped fresh cilantro

½ cup (125 mL) extra virgin olive oil

1 tbsp (15 mL) liquid honey

Grated zest and freshly squeezed juice of 1 lime

Salt and freshly ground black pepper

1 In a large bowl, toss together green onions, mangos, lettuce, red pepper and cabbage.

2 In a jar with a tight-fitting lid, combine cilantro, oil, honey, lime zest and lime juice. Add to mango mixture and toss gently to coat. Let stand for 10 minutes to allow the flavors to develop.

TIPS

When it comes to mangos, color is not an indication of freshness. Instead of looking at color, choose fruit that is slightly soft to the touch. Store unripe mangos at room temperature. Once they are ripe, store them in the refrigerator for up to 5 days.

Slicing a mango can be a challenge. First, slice the unpeeled mango from stem end to bottom end, parallel to the flat seed. Flip the mango around and repeat on the other side. These slices are known as cheeks. (What's left in the middle is mostly the seed.) Placing the cheeks flesh side up, cut parallel slices into the flesh, being careful not to cut through to the skin. Turn the mango 90 degrees and cut another set of parallel slices, making a checkerboard pattern. Turn the scored cheek inside out by pushing the skin up from underneath. Using a sharp paring knife, scrape the chunks off the skin.

GINGER PORK WRAPS

SERVES 6 | 4- TO 6-QUART SLOW COOKER

These wraps combine the flavors of sweet-and-sour pork with crisp vegetables. Everyone will be asking for seconds.

¼ cup (60 mL) hoisin sauce	**1** In a bowl, combine hoisin sauce, ginger and honey.
3 tbsp (45 mL) grated gingerroot	
3 tbsp (45 mL) liquid honey	**2** Place pork roast in slow cooker stoneware and brush with sauce to coat completely.
1 boneless pork loin rib end roast (about 2½ lbs/1.25 kg), trimmed of excess fat	
2½ cups (625 mL) shredded cabbage	**3** Cover and cook on Low for 8 to 10 hours or on High for 4 to 5 hours, until meat is very tender.
½ cup (125 mL) shredded carrot	
3 green onions, finely chopped	**4** Transfer pork to a bowl and, using two forks, pull meat into shreds. Skim fat from sauce. Return meat to slow cooker.
2 tbsp (30 mL) rice vinegar	
10 to 12 10-inch (25 cm) flour tortillas	**5** In a bowl, combine cabbage, carrot, green onions and vinegar.

6 Wrap tortillas in foil and heat in a preheated 350°F (180°C) oven for 10 minutes. To serve, spread about ⅓ cup (75 mL) pork mixture down center of each warm tortilla. Top with ¼ cup (50 mL) cabbage mixture. Roll up each tortilla tightly.

TIP

If you are pressed for time, look for pre-packaged coleslaw mix to use in place of the cabbage and carrot (use about 3½ cups/875 mL).

FRESH GINGERROOT

There is no need to peel gingerroot before grating. Use a standard kitchen grater with fine holes. Wrap any unused ginger in plastic wrap and freeze. Frozen gingerroot can be grated without defrosting.

PORK CARNITAS

SERVES 10 TO 12 | 6- TO 8-QUART SLOW COOKER

Enter any taqueria in California and you'll find carnitas on the menu, usually pork shoulder (butt) roast, slow-braised, pulled apart, then roasted over high heat to caramelize it. This is a great way to use the slow cooker and the oven to create a Mexican dish to feed a crowd. Add some sangría or margaritas, and you'll have a party-in-a-pot!

• Rimmed baking sheet

4 lbs (2 kg) boneless pork shoulder blade (butt) roast, trimmed and cut into large cubes

8 cloves garlic, minced

1 tsp (5 mL) salt

½ tsp (2 mL) freshly ground black pepper

8 cups (2 L) water

1 cup (250 mL) freshly squeezed orange juice

2 tbsp (30 mL) olive oil

1 can (14 oz/398 mL) refried beans, warmed (optional)

20 to 24 6- or 7-inch (15 or 18 cm) corn or flour tortillas, warmed

Fresh cilantro leaves

1 large white onion, thinly sliced

4 avocados, peeled and diced

20 to 24 lime wedges

1 In slow cooker stoneware, combine pork, garlic, salt, pepper and water.

2 Cover and cook on Low for 10 to 12 hours or on High for 5 to 6 hours, until pork is fork-tender. Discard cooking liquid.

3 Preheat oven to 400°F (200°C). Break pork into smaller chunks and spread on baking sheet. Drizzle with orange juice and oil. Roast, stirring occasionally, for 15 to 20 minutes or until browned and crisp.

4 Spread a layer of refried beans (if using) on each tortilla. Top with pork, cilantro, onion and avocado. Serve with a lime wedge to squeeze over top.

MAKE AHEAD This dish can be assembled up to 12 hours in advance. Prepare through step 1, cover and refrigerate overnight. The next day, place stoneware in slow cooker and proceed with step 2.

TIP

Carnitas means "little meats," a type of Mexican braised or roasted pork. Carnitas are sometimes served with refried beans and thinly sliced radishes. You can add the radishes to this recipe, if you choose.

PULLED PORK SANDWICHES WITH RADISH SLAW

SERVES 8 TO 10 | 6- TO 8-QUART SLOW COOKER

Forget any worries about feeding a large crowd when you make this slow cooker all-time favorite. It starts with a dry rub to season the meat, then slow-cooks it in tangy apple juice to tenderize it. A Habitat for Humanity group conducting a local build were the lucky recipients of my recipe test, and everyone gave it a "hammers up" rating!

¼ cup (60 mL) garlic powder

¼ cup (60 mL) paprika

2 tbsp (30 mL) chili powder

2 tbsp (30 mL) dried oregano

2 tbsp (30 mL) coarse salt

1 tbsp (15 mL) freshly ground black pepper

1 tbsp (15 mL) celery seeds

3 lbs (1.5 kg) boneless pork shoulder blade (butt) roast, trimmed

1 large onion, sliced

5 cloves garlic, minced

4 sprigs fresh thyme

1 bay leaf

2 cups (500 mL) unsweetened apple juice

BARBECUE SAUCE

½ cup (125 mL) smoky-flavored barbecue sauce

1 tbsp (15 mL) tomato paste

1 clove garlic, minced

1 chipotle pepper in adobo sauce, minced (optional)

Radish Slaw (see recipe, opposite)

24 small hamburger buns, toasted

1 In a small bowl, combine garlic powder, paprika, chili powder, oregano, salt, pepper and celery seeds. Place pork in a bowl and rub all over with spice mixture. Let marinate at room temperature for 15 to 30 minutes.

2 Arrange onion over bottom of slow cooker stoneware. Place pork on top. Add garlic, thyme, bay leaf and apple juice.

3 Cover and cook on Low for 8 to 10 hours or on High for 4 to 6 hours, until pork is fork-tender and falling apart. Transfer pork to a cutting board and let cool slightly.

4 Remove any butcher's string holding the roast together. Using two forks, shred pork.

5 Skim fat from cooking liquid. Reserve 1 cup (250 mL) cooking liquid and set aside. Discard bay leaf and the remaining cooking liquid. Return pork to stoneware.

6 **SAUCE:** In a bowl, combine the reserved cooking liquid, barbecue sauce, tomato paste, garlic and chipotle pepper (if using). Stir into pork. Keep warm on Low heat.

7 Spoon pork mixture on the bottom half of each bun and top with a big scoop of slaw. Cover with top half of bun.

8 Divide potatoes evenly among individual serving plates. Ladle pork mixture on top and top with cheese curds and parsley. Serve immediately.

MAKE AHEAD This dish can be assembled up to 2 days in advance, as long as the pork is left out. Complete steps 1, 3 and 4. Cover and refrigerate. When ready to cook, add vegetable oil to the skillet and brown the pork as directed in step 2. Place stoneware in slow cooker, add pork and proceed with step 5.

TIPS

While many pork dishes use chicken broth to make the gravy, I like to use beef broth for this one, to add richness. For a lighter-flavored gravy, you can use chicken or veal broth.

Broth (or stock) is one of the most indispensable pantry staples. Commercial broth cubes and powders are loaded with salt and just don't deliver the flavor of homemade stock or prepared broth. I like to keep 32-oz (1 L) Tetra Paks on hand, especially the sodium-reduced variety.

VARIATIONS

This recipe also works well with beef. Use a braising roast, such as a blade, cross rib, chuck or shoulder, and cut it into 1-inch (2.5 cm) cubes.

Reduce the beef broth to 1 cup (250 mL) and add $\frac{1}{2}$ cup (125 mL) dry red wine.

For an upscale version of the poutine, use a soft melting cheese, such as Brie, cut into chunks.

INDONESIAN PORK SATAY STEW

SERVES 4 TO 6 | 4- TO 6-QUART SLOW COOKER

Satay is an Indonesian specialty of spicy marinated meat that is skewered, then broiled or grilled. Here I've taken all the great flavors of a pork satay and created a lively stew.

2 tbsp (30 mL) all-purpose flour

½ tsp (2 mL) salt

½ tsp (2 mL) freshly ground black pepper

2 lbs (1 kg) boneless pork shoulder blade (butt), cut into 1-inch (2.5 cm) cubes

2 tbsp (30 mL) vegetable oil (approx.)

2 red or green bell peppers, cut into 1-inch (2.5 cm) pieces

1 large red onion, cut into wedges

1 cup (250 mL) thick and chunky salsa (mild or hot)

½ cup (125 mL) creamy peanut butter

1 tbsp (15 mL) soy sauce

1 tbsp (15 mL) freshly squeezed lime juice

1½ tsp (7 mL) grated gingerroot

½ tsp (2 mL) ground turmeric

½ tsp (2 mL) ground coriander

½ cup (125 mL) light (5%) cream or evaporated milk

1 tbsp (15 mL) cornstarch

3 cups (750 mL) hot cooked white or brown rice

⅓ cup (75 mL) chopped dry-roasted peanuts

2 green onions, sliced

1 In a heavy plastic bag, combine flour, salt and pepper. In batches, add pork to bag and toss to coat with flour mixture. Discard excess flour mixture.

2 In a large nonstick skillet, heat half the oil over medium-high heat. Cook pork in batches, adding more oil as needed, for about 4 minutes or until browned all over. Using a slotted spoon, transfer to slow cooker stoneware.

3 Stir in bell peppers, red onion, salsa, peanut butter, soy sauce, lime juice, ginger, turmeric and coriander.

4 Cover and cook on Low for 8 to 10 hours or on High for 4 to 6 hours, until pork is tender.

5 In a jar with a tight-fitting lid, combine cream and cornstarch; shake until blended. Stir into stew. Cover and cook on High for 10 to 15 minutes or until sauce has thickened.

6 Divide rice among bowls and ladle stew over top. Garnish with peanuts and green onions.

MAKE AHEAD Combine the ingredients in step 3 in the stone cooker stoneware. Cover and refrigerate overnight. The next day, dredge and brown the pork as directed in steps 1 and 2. Place stoneware in slow cooker, add pork and proceed with step 4.

TIPS

Grating gingerroot is easiest if you keep a nub of it in the freezer. (Ginger tends to get moldy and soft too quickly when it's stored in the refrigerator.) Use a Microplane-style grater for best results. Microplanes have tiny razor-like edges that make quick and easy tasks of both grating and cleaning. You will find Microplanes in good kitchenware and department stores.

To store gingerroot, peel it and place it in a jar with a tight-fitting lid. Add enough sherry to cover. The sherry will saturate and preserve the ginger. Refrigerate for up to 1 month.

When browning meat in hot oil, avoid overfilling the skillet. If the pan is too full, the meat will steam rather than brown. Turn the meat frequently and cook it as quickly as possible, then use a slotted spoon to remove it.

PUMPKIN-SPICED PORK STEW

SERVES 4 TO 6 | 4- TO 6-QUART SLOW COOKER

This delicious stew is full of cozy fall flavors. Tender chunks of pork combined with sweet potatoes and apples are simmered in a savory gravy that is spiked with the fragrant smells of cinnamon, nutmeg and cloves. It's a true family favorite.

2 large sweet onions, chopped

2 cloves garlic, minced

¼ cup (60 mL) all-purpose flour

1 tsp (5 mL) salt

¼ tsp (1 mL) freshly ground black pepper

3 lbs (1.5 kg) boneless pork shoulder blade (butt), trimmed and cut into 1-inch (2.5 cm) cubes

2 tbsp (30 mL) vegetable oil (approx.)

1 tbsp (15 mL) butter

1 can (19 oz/540 mL) tomatoes, with juice

1 sweet potato, chopped

1 Granny Smith or other tart apple, chopped

3 tbsp (45 mL) dried currants

½ tsp (2 mL) pumpkin pie spice

¼ tsp (1 mL) ground cumin

1 bay leaf

TOPPING

1½ cups (375 mL) plain yogurt

½ cup (125 mL) chopped green onions

1 Layer onions and garlic in slow cooker stoneware.

2 In a heavy plastic bag, combine flour, salt and pepper. In batches, add pork to bag and toss to coat with flour mixture. Discard excess flour mixture.

3 In a large nonstick skillet, heat half the oil and the butter over medium-high heat. Cook pork in batches, adding oil as needed, for about 4 minutes or until browned all over. Using a slotted spoon, transfer to stoneware.

4 Stir in tomatoes with juice, sweet potato, apple, currants, pumpkin pie spice, cumin and bay leaf.

5 Cover and cook on Low for 8 to 10 hours or on High for 4 to 5 hours, until pork is tender. Discard bay leaf.

6 In a bowl, combine yogurt and green onions. Ladle stew into individual serving bowls and top each with a dollop of yogurt mixture.

MAKE AHEAD This dish can be assembled up to 12 hours in advance, as long as the pork is left out. Complete step 1, skip over steps 2 and 3, then complete step 4. Cover and refrigerate overnight. The next day, dredge and brown the pork as directed in steps 2 and 3. Place stoneware in slow cooker, add pork and proceed with step 4.

TIPS

To avoid tears when chopping onions, put the onions in the freezer for a few minutes first.

You can make your own pumpkin pie spice using 1 tbsp (15 mL) ground cinnamon and $\frac{1}{4}$ tsp (1 mL) each ground ginger, nutmeg and cloves.

Cooking times can vary a great deal between slow cooker manufacturers. Always let your food cook for the minimum amount of time before testing for doneness.

SWEET ONIONS

There are several varieties of sweet onions, including Vidalia, Walla Walla, Maui and Sweetie Sweet. Although all onions have natural sugars, sweet onions have a lower sulfur content and higher water content, which emphasizes their sweetness and makes them less pungent.

NORTH AFRICAN LAMB TAGINE

SERVES 4 TO 6 | 4- TO 6-QUART SLOW COOKER

The stews of North Africa are traditionally made in a conical vessel called a tagine. The lid of the tagine is tall, and it causes the steam to build up and precipitate back down to the stew so that none of the aroma or flavor is lost during cooking. The slow cooker uses basically the same principal. Crunchy peanut butter thickens the broth at the end of the cooking time, and the couscous soaks up the wonderful flavors.

2 tbsp (30 mL) vegetable oil (approx.)

2 lbs (1 kg) boneless stewing lamb, cut into 1-inch (2.5 cm) cubes

4 parsnips, diced

2 sweet potatoes, peeled and diced

1 onion, finely chopped

4 cloves garlic, finely chopped

1 tbsp (15 mL) curry powder

½ tsp (2 mL) ground cumin

¼ tsp (1 mL) ground allspice

1 cup (250 mL) beef broth

1 can (14 oz/398 mL) diced tomatoes, with juices

1 3-inch (7.5 cm) cinnamon stick

½ tsp (2 mL) hot pepper flakes

2 tbsp (30 mL) crunchy peanut butter

Salt

Hot cooked couscous

Chopped fresh parsley or cilantro

1 In a large skillet, heat half the oil over medium-high heat. Cook lamb in batches, adding more oil as needed, for 4 minutes or until browned all over. Using a slotted spoon, transfer to slow cooker stoneware, leaving fat in pan.

2 Reduce heat to medium-low. Add parsnips, sweet potatoes and onion to skillet and sauté for about 4 minutes or until starting to soften. Add garlic, curry powder, cumin and allspice; sauté for about 1 minute or until vegetables are coated and spices are fragrant. Using a slotted spoon, transfer to stoneware.

3 Add broth to skillet and bring to a boil, scraping up any brown bits from pan. Pour over lamb mixture. Stir in tomatoes with juices, cinnamon stick and hot pepper flakes.

4 Cover and cook on Low for 6 to 8 hours or on High for 3 to 4 hours, until lamb is tender and stew is bubbling.

5 Discard cinnamon stick. Stir in peanut butter until thoroughly combined. Season to taste with salt.

6 Place couscous on a serving platter. Top with stew and sprinkle with parsley.

TIPS

For the best flavor, start with whole cumin seeds and allspice berries. Toast them in a dry skillet over medium-high heat, stirring constantly, for about 3 minutes or until fragrant. Then grind them as finely as you can in a spice grinder or using a mortar and pestle.

When browning meat in hot oil, avoid overfilling the skillet. If the pan is too full, the meat will steam rather than brown. Turn the meat frequently and cook it as quickly as possible, then use a slotted spoon to remove it.

The flavors really mingle by the second day, so don't be afraid to cook this stew one day, pop it in the refrigerator, then reheat and eat it the next day.

COUSCOUS

Couscous, a North African granular pasta, is available in a precooked instant form in most grocery stores. Unless the box instructions tell you otherwise, for 4 servings, bring 1½ cups (375 mL) water to a boil, then stir in 1 cup (250 mL) couscous. Cover, remove from heat and let stand for 5 minutes. Fluff with a fork, then stir in chopped fresh cilantro or parsley. Couscous, enlivened with any fresh herb, is a good complement for most stews.

INDIAN LAMB CURRY

SERVES 4 TO 6 | 4- TO 6-QUART SLOW COOKER

Accompany this sweet and flavorful curry with additional sweet mango chutney and a selection of condiments — chopped green onions, chopped peanuts and toasted coconut. It's best served on a bed of sweet-scented basmati, a long-grain East Indian rice.

2 tbsp (30 mL) vegetable oil (approx.)

1 lamb shank or butt roast (about 2 lbs/1 kg), well trimmed and cut into 1-inch (2.5 cm) cubes

2 tbsp (30 mL) all-purpose flour

2 tbsp (30 mL) curry powder

½ tsp (2 mL) hot pepper flakes

½ tsp (2 mL) paprika

½ tsp (2 mL) dried marjoram

1 cup (250 mL) chicken broth

2 large Granny Smith apples, peeled and coarsely chopped

2 stalks celery, coarsely chopped

2 onions, finely chopped

2 cloves garlic, minced

1 tbsp (15 mL) minced gingerroot

1 can (14 oz/398 mL) coconut milk

1 tsp (5 mL) salt

¼ cup (60 mL) mango chutney

½ cup (125 mL) raisins

⅓ cup (75 mL) plain yogurt or sour cream

1 tsp (5 mL) grated lemon zest

1 In a large nonstick skillet, heat half the oil over medium-high heat. Cook lamb in batches, adding more oil as needed, until browned all over. Return all lamb to skillet.

2 In a small bowl, combine flour, curry powder, hot pepper flakes, paprika and marjoram. Sprinkle over lamb cubes, tossing to coat well. Add broth and cook, scraping up brown bits from bottom of skillet. Bring to a boil, reduce heat and simmer for about 5 minutes.

3 Transfer meat mixture to slow cooker stoneware. Add apples, celery, onions, garlic, ginger, coconut milk and salt.

4 Cover and cook on Low for 8 to 10 hours or on High for 4 to 6 hours, until meat is tender.

5 Transfer curry to a serving dish. Stir in chutney, raisins, yogurt and lemon zest. Serve immediately.

MAKE AHEAD This dish can be assembled up to 12 hours in advance. Prepare the ingredients as directed up to the cooking stage, (but without adding chutney, raisins and lemon zest), and refrigerate in stoneware insert overnight. The next day, place stone-ware in slow cooker and continue cooking as directed.

TIPS

Mango chutney is found in the condiment section of most supermarkets.

Canned coconut milk is made from grated and soaked coconut pulp — not, as you might think, from the liquid found inside the coconut. It can be found in the Asian foods section of most supermarkets or Asian food stores. Be sure you don't buy coconut cream, which is often used for making tropical drinks such as piña coladas, and is far too sweet for curry.

CURRY POWDER

Curry powder, a blend of more than 20 herbs, seeds and spices, is integral to Indian cuisine (in India, most cooks blend their own mixtures). Cardamom, chilies, cinnamon, coriander, cumin, fennel, mace, pepper, poppy and sesame seeds and saffron are common curry seasonings. Turmeric gives curry its distinctive yellow color.

Curry paste can be used instead of curry powder. It comes in different heat levels, so buy a mild version if you don't like your curry too hot.

To eliminate the raw taste of curry powder and sweeten the spice, sauté it in a dry skillet before using. Cook for about 30 seconds, or just until fragrant.

PROVENÇAL LAMB STEW

SERVES 4 | 4- TO 6-QUART SLOW COOKER

This stew is full of flavors from the south of France, and is one of those dishes that tastes even better the day after it is made. Serve it over a heaping mound of garlic mashed potatoes, with a simple steamed green vegetable, such as fresh green beans.

2 tbsp (30 mL) all-purpose flour

½ tsp (2 mL) salt

¼ tsp (1 mL) freshly ground black pepper

1½ lbs (750 g) boneless lamb shoulder, trimmed and cut into 1-inch (2.5 cm) cubes

2 tbsp (30 mL) olive oil (approx.)

2 onions, chopped

2 cloves garlic, minced

1 carrot, chopped

1 stalk celery, chopped

½ cup (125 mL) dry white wine

1 can (19 oz/540 mL) tomatoes, drained and chopped

2 cups (500 mL) cooked or canned white kidney beans (see page 16), drained and rinsed

½ cup (125 mL) chicken broth

1 tbsp (15 mL) chopped fresh rosemary

1 bay leaf

Chopped fresh parsley

1 In a heavy plastic bag, combine flour, salt and pepper. In batches, add lamb to bag and toss to coat with flour mixture. Discard excess flour mixture.

2 In a large nonstick skillet, heat half the oil over medium-high heat. Cook lamb in batches, adding more oil as needed, for 5 minutes or until browned all over. Using a slotted spoon, transfer to slow cooker stoneware. Sprinkle with onions, garlic, carrot and celery.

3 Add wine to the skillet and bring to a boil, scraping up any brown bits from pan. Pour over lamb mixture. Stir in tomatoes, beans, broth, rosemary and bay leaf.

4 Cover and cook on Low for 8 to 10 hours or on High for 4 to 5 hours, until lamb and vegetables are tender and stew is bubbling. Discard bay leaf. Season to taste with salt and pepper. Serve garnished with parsley.

MAKE AHEAD In slow cooker stoneware, combine onions, garlic, carrot, celery, wine, tomatoes, beans, broth, rosemary and bay leaf. Cover and refrigerate overnight. The next day, dredge and brown the lamb as directed in steps 1 and 2. Place stoneware in slow cooker, add lamb and proceed with step 4.

TIPS

If you are not a lamb fan, you can substitute cubes of lean pork shoulder blade (butt) or stewing beef.

The best cuts for lamb stew come from the shoulder or shank. Avoid using lamb loin — it can be very expensive and will overcook quickly.

MEDITERRANEAN PULLED LAMB WITH COUSCOUS

SERVES 6 TO 8 | 4- TO 6-QUART SLOW COOKER

I love the flavor combination of lemon, garlic and herbs with lamb, and this recipe fulfills my taste buds' expectations! This is not meant to be a roast, but it is meant to be fall-apart soft — almost like "pulled" lamb. I serve it over Greek-Style Couscous (see recipe, opposite), but if you're pressed for time, a plain couscous served with a tomato and cucumber salad will work well too.

1 boneless lamb shoulder roast (3 to 4 lbs/1.5 to 2 kg), tied

½ tsp (2 mL) salt

¼ tsp (1 mL) freshly ground black pepper

4 to 6 cloves garlic, crushed

½ cup (125 mL) freshly squeezed lemon juice

¼ cup (60 mL) olive oil

1 tsp (5 mL) dried oregano

1 tsp (5 mL) ground nutmeg

MINT VINEGAR

¼ cup (60 mL) white balsamic vinegar

1 tbsp (15 mL) finely chopped fresh mint leaves

1 tsp (5 mL) granulated sugar

Couscous (see recipe, opposite)

1 Place lamb in slow cooker stoneware and sprinkle with salt and pepper.

2 In a bowl, combine garlic, lemon juice, oil, oregano and nutmeg. Pour over lamb.

3 Cover and cook on Low for 10 to 12 hours or on High for 5 to 6 hours, until lamb is fork-tender. Transfer lamb to a bowl and cut off strings. Using two forks, pull lamb apart into chunky shreds, discarding excess fat. Arrange on a deep serving platter.

4 **VINEGAR:** In a small saucepan, combine vinegar, mint and sugar; bring to a boil. Reduce heat and simmer, stirring, for 1 minute or until sugar is dissolved. Drizzle over lamb. Serve with couscous alongside.

TIPS

Fresh lamb shoulder roasts are sometimes hard to find if you don't have a farmer's market nearby. Ask your butcher to order it in for you, if possible, or look for a frozen roast and thaw it in the refrigerator (it'll take 1 to 2 days).

Fresh mint in the vinegar is what really elevates this lamb dish and finishes it beautifully. I would not recommend substituting dried mint. Take the extra time to chop the fresh herb. Look for small containers of fresh herbs in the produce aisle of the supermarket.

COUSCOUS

SERVES 8

Using all the flavors and ingredients of a Greek salad, this hearty side dish is a perfect accompaniment for the pulled lamb.

1½ cups (375 mL) water

1 cup (250 mL) couscous

¼ cup (60 mL) extra virgin olive oil

2 tbsp (30 mL) freshly squeezed lemon juice

1 tsp (5 mL) dried oregano

1 tomato, chopped

2 cups (500 mL) coarsely chopped cucumber

½ cup (125 mL) crumbled feta cheese

½ cup (125 mL) coarsely chopped pitted black olives

Salt and freshly ground black pepper

1 In a saucepan, bring water to a boil over high heat. Stir in couscous. Remove from heat, cover and let stand for about 5 minutes or until liquid is absorbed.

2 Meanwhile, in a bowl, whisk together oil, lemon juice and oregano. Add tomato, cucumber, cheese and olives. Add couscous and gently toss to coat. Season to taste with salt and pepper.

TIP

To get the most juice from a lemon, let it warm to room temperature, then roll it on the counter, pressing down with the palm of your hand, before squeezing it.

VEGAN

TEX-MEX TOMATO RICE SOUP

SERVES 6 | 4- TO 6-QUART SLOW COOKER

Garnish this kid-friendly soup with minced fresh cilantro and/or vegan sour cream. Serve alongside quesadillas for an easy dinner.

2 tbsp (30 mL) vegetable oil

2 cloves garlic, minced

1 onion, chopped

1 jalapeño pepper, seeded and minced

½ tsp (2 mL) ground cumin

¼ tsp (1 mL) chili powder

2 carrots, chopped

1 cup (250 mL) frozen corn kernels, thawed

¼ cup (60 mL) long-grain white rice

1 can (28 oz/796 mL) diced tomatoes, with juices

3 cups (750 mL) water

¼ cup (60 mL) minced fresh cilantro (optional)

1 tbsp (15 mL) freshly squeezed lime juice

Salt and freshly ground black pepper

Vegan sour cream (optional)

1 In a large skillet, heat oil over medium-high heat. Sauté garlic, onion, jalapeño, cumin and chili powder for about 5 minutes or until onion is tender and translucent. Transfer to slow cooker stoneware. Stir in carrots, corn, rice, tomatoes with juices and water.

2 Cover and cook on Low for 6 to 8 hours or on High for 3 to 4 hours, until soup is bubbling and rice is tender. Stir in cilantro (if using) and lime juice. Season to taste with salt and pepper. Top with vegan sour cream (if using).

TIP

Add some crumbled corn tortillas for added crunch.

RED BEAN & BARLEY SOUP

SERVES 6 TO 8 | 4- TO 6-QUART SLOW COOKER

On a car trip home from Florida one year, we stumbled upon the quaint Cathedral Café in Fayetteville, West Virginia. My daughter ordered this soup and enjoyed it so much that I just had to ask for the recipe.

4 cups (1 L) cooked or canned red kidney beans (see page 16), drained and rinsed

1 onion, finely chopped

1 green bell pepper, finely chopped

1 cup (250 mL) finely chopped carrots

1 cup (250 mL) finely chopped celery

1 cup (250 mL) pearl barley, rinsed

1½ tsp (7 mL) dried basil

¼ tsp (1 mL) freshly ground black pepper

4 cups (1 L) vegetable broth

1 can (19 oz/540 mL) diced tomatoes, with juices

1 cup (250 mL) prepared tomato pasta sauce

¼ cup (60 mL) chopped fresh parsley

1 In slow cooker stoneware, combine beans, onion, green pepper, carrots, celery, barley, basil, pepper, broth, tomatoes with juices and pasta sauce.

2 Cover and cook on Low for 6 to 8 hours or on High for 3 to 4 hours, until soup is bubbling and barley is tender.

3 Ladle into bowls and garnish with parsley.

TIP

To avoid tears when chopping onions, put the onions in the freezer for a few minutes first.

RED LENTIL & APPLE SOUP

SERVES 4 TO 6 | 4- TO 6-QUART SLOW COOKER

Don't worry about any overwhelming spiciness here. This surprisingly sweet tasting soup will warm you to your toes.

4 carrots, diced

2 stalks celery, diced

1 large onion, diced

1 Granny Smith apple, peeled and diced

1 tbsp (15 mL) grated gingerroot

1 large clove garlic, minced

1 tbsp (15 mL) curry powder

¾ tsp (3 mL) ground cumin or cumin seeds

4 cups (1 L) vegetable broth

½ cup (125 mL) dried red lentils, rinsed (see tip, below)

Plain vegan yogurt

Toasted whole wheat pitas

1 In slow cooker stoneware, combine carrots, celery, onion, apple, ginger, garlic, curry, cumin, broth and lentils; stir to mix well.

2 Cover and cook on Low for 8 to 10 hours or on High for 4 to 6 hours, until thick and bubbling.

3 Transfer mixture in batches to a blender or food processor and process until smooth. Return to slow cooker and process to keep warm.

4 Ladle soup into individual bowls and top each with a dollop of yogurt. Serve with whole wheat pitas.

MAKE AHEAD This soup can be assembled 12 to 24 hours in advance. Follow preparation directions and refrigerate overnight in slow cooker stoneware. The next day, place stoneware in slow cooker and cook as directed.

TIP

Red lentils are available in cans, but the dried variety cook up so fast that they're the better (and cheaper) choice. It is important to pick over lentils to remove any sticks or broken pieces, then rinse and drain before using. If the holes in your strainer are too large, line it with a paper towel before rinsing.

BARBECUE TOFU SANDWICHES

SERVES 4 TO 6 | 4- TO 6-QUART SLOW COOKER, STONEWARE GREASED

A friend of mine said that barbecue sauce is the one thing she misses now that she is a vegetarian, since it's typically eaten with steak or chicken. I decided to try to satisfy her craving by creating a tasty barbecue tofu dish made in the slow cooker. She loved the recipe and has added it to her slow cooker repertoire. Use extra-firm tofu in the slow cooker, so it will retain its texture. You won't believe your taste buds.

2 packages (each 14 oz/420 g) extra-firm or dry-style tofu

2 cloves garlic, minced

¼ cup (60 mL) firmly packed brown sugar

1 tbsp (15 mL) chili powder

1 tsp (5 mL) paprika or smoked paprika

1 can (7½ oz/221 mL) prepared tomato sauce

1 cup (250 mL) ketchup

2 tbsp (30 mL) soy sauce

2 tbsp (30 mL) freshly squeezed lemon juice

2 tbsp (30 mL) Dijon mustard

4 to 6 panini rolls or ciabatta buns

Baby arugula or shredded lettuce

Sautéed onion slices

1 If using extra-firm tofu, slice each block into four ¾-inch (2 cm) slabs. Line a baking sheet with a triple layer of paper towels. Arrange tofu slabs in a single layer on top. Cover tofu with another triple layer of paper towels, then place another baking sheet on top and weigh it down with unopened canned goods. Let stand for 15 minutes to 1 hour to press out extra liquid. (If using dry-style tofu, no pressing is necessary.)

2 In a large bowl, combine garlic, brown sugar, chili powder, paprika, tomato sauce, ketchup, soy sauce, lemon juice and mustard.

3 Cut tofu into cubes and place in prepared slow cooker stoneware. Pour sauce over tofu and toss gently to coat.

4 Cover and cook on High for 2 to 3 hours or on Low for 4 to 6 hours, until hot and fragrant.

5 Split rolls in half lengthwise. Pile arugula on bottom halves and spoon tofu mixture over arugula. Top with onion slices and cover with top halves. Serve immediately.

TIPS

Because tofu has a sponge-like consistency, it absorbs the flavors of any sauce in which it is marinated.

Smoked paprika is made by grinding peppers that have undergone a smoking process. You can find it in various heat levels (from mild to hot). Be careful how much you use, because smoky seasonings can easily overpower the flavor of a dish.

BUYING TOFU

There are many types of tofu available, but the type that works best for this recipe is labeled "extra-firm" or "super-firm." Much of the liquid has already been pressed out of it, but you need to press out the rest or your tofu will just melt into the sauce. I prefer to use "dry-style tofu," which doesn't require the pressing step; look for it in Asian supermarkets.

SAUCY LENTIL SPOON BURGERS

SERVES 8 | 4- TO 6-QUART SLOW COOKER

This is a yummy vegan twist on a family favorite. For a Middle Eastern flair, stuff these lentils into pita breads lined with lettuce leaves. The lettuce helps to keep the lentils from soaking the bread.

1 cup (250 mL) dried lentils, rinsed and sorted

2 cups (500 mL) water

1½ cups (375 mL) finely chopped celery

1½ cups (375 mL) finely chopped carrots

1 large onion, finely chopped

¾ cup (175 mL) ketchup

2 tbsp (30 mL) packed brown sugar

2 tbsp (30 mL) Worcestershire sauce

2 tbsp (30 mL) cider vinegar

8 kaiser buns, halved and lightly toasted

8 slices vegan Cheddar cheese (optional)

1 In a saucepan, combine lentils and water. Bring to a boil and reduce heat. Cover and simmer for 10 minutes. Transfer lentils and water to slow cooker stoneware.

2 Add celery, carrots, onion, ketchup, brown sugar and Worcestershire sauce to slow cooker; stir to combine.

3 Cover and cook on Low for 10 to 12 hours or on High for 4 to 6 hours, until lentils are tender. Just before serving, stir in vinegar.

4 Spoon ½ cup (125 mL) filling onto bottoms of toasted kaisers. Top with vegan Cheddar (if using) and top halves of buns.

TIP

Lentils are an inexpensive source of protein, as well as being high in fiber, complex carbohydrates and B vitamins. It's best to use green or brown lentils for this recipe since they'll hold their shape. Smaller red or yellow lentils are better suited for soups.

HEARTY VEGETABLE CHILI

SERVES 6 | 4- TO 6-QUART SLOW COOKER

This dish is a spicy blend of squash, carrots, black beans and more — you'll never miss the meat!

1 medium-sized butternut squash, peeled and cut into ¾-inch (2 cm) cubes

2 carrots, diced

1 onion, finely chopped

1 can (28 oz/796 mL) diced tomatoes, with juices

2 cans (each 19 oz/540 mL) black beans, drained and rinsed, or 4 cups (1 L) home-cooked beans (see page 16)

1 can (4½ oz/127 mL) chopped green chilies, with liquid

1 cup (250 mL) vegetable broth

3 tbsp (45 mL) chili powder

½ tsp (2 mL) salt

¼ cup (60 mL) chopped fresh cilantro, plus more for serving

Vegan sour cream

1 In slow cooker stoneware, combine squash, carrots, onion, tomatoes with juices, black beans, chilies with liquid, broth, chili powder and salt; stir to mix well.

2 Cover and cook on Low for 6 to 8 hours or on High for 3 to 4 hours, until hot and bubbling.

3 Add cilantro; cover and cook on High for 15 to 20 minutes longer.

4 Spoon into serving bowls and top with a dollop of vegan sour cream and additional chopped fresh cilantro.

MAKE AHEAD This chili can be assembled 12 hours in advance of cooking. Follow preparation directions and refrigerate overnight in slow cooker stoneware. The next day, place stoneware in slow cooker and continue cooking as directed.

TIPS

You can substitute 2 large sweet potatoes (peeled and chopped) for the squash.

Canned green chilies are found in the Mexican food section of the supermarket. They are sold whole or chopped.

MUSHROOM RAGOÛT WITH POLENTA

SERVES 4 TO 6 | 4- TO 6-QUART SLOW COOKER

Portobello mushrooms give this versatile dish a rich, robust flavor and an almost meaty texture. It's a popular main course even among diehard meat eaters.

- Baking sheet, lined with parchment paper

2 tbsp (30 mL) olive oil

1 onion, finely chopped

2 cloves garlic, finely chopped

1 lb (500 g) white or cremini mushrooms, sliced

8 oz (250 g) portobello mushroom caps, thinly sliced

½ tsp (2 mL) dried rosemary or tarragon

Pinch hot pepper flakes

½ cup (125 mL) vegetable broth

1 tbsp (15 mL) balsamic vinegar

Salt and freshly ground black pepper

¼ cup (60 mL) chopped fresh parsley

Vegan Parmesan cheese

GRILLED POLENTA

1 tube (1 lb/500 g) plain prepared polenta

Olive oil

Salt and freshly ground black pepper

1 In a nonstick skillet, heat oil over medium-high heat. Sauté onion for 3 to 4 minutes or until tender and translucent. Add garlic and sauté for 1 minute. Transfer to slow cooker stoneware.

2 Stir in white mushrooms, portobello mushrooms, rosemary, hot pepper flakes and broth.

3 Cover and cook on Low for 6 to 8 hours or on High for 3 to 4 hours, until mushrooms are tender. Stir in balsamic vinegar. Season to taste with salt and black pepper.

4 **POLENTA:** Meanwhile, preheat broiler. Using a sharp knife, cut polenta into ½-inch (1 cm) slices. Place on prepared baking sheet and brush tops with oil. Broil 6 to 8 inches (15 to 20 cm) from heat, without turning, for 10 to 15 minutes or until golden and just starting to brown. Season to taste with salt and pepper. Arrange on a serving plate.

5 Ladle mushroom mixture over polenta and garnish with parsley and vegan Parmesan.

MAKE AHEAD This dish can be assembled up to 24 hours in advance. Prepare through step 2, cover and refrigerate overnight. The next day, place stoneware in slow cooker and proceed with step 3.

TIPS

Store mushrooms in a paper bag, with the top loosely folded over once or twice, or place them in a glass container and cover it with a tea towel or moist paper towel. Be sure to allow air circulation. Store in the refrigerator (but not in the crisper) and use within a few days — or a week, if they are packaged and unopened.

To prepare mushrooms, first trim off the bottoms of the stems, then wipe off the mushrooms. Don't rinse or soak the mushrooms, or they'll absorb water and turn mushy when you cook them.

Polenta is the name given to both the popular Italian dish of cornmeal mush and the cornmeal used to make the dish.

VARIATION

The mushroom mixture could also be served over hot cooked rice or pasta.

LENTIL CURRY WITH SQUASH & CASHEWS

SERVES 6 | 4- TO 6-QUART SLOW COOKER

For the vegan in the family or for adding to your array of meatless entrées, try this Middle Eastern–inspired dish.

2 tsp (10 mL) vegetable oil

1 onion, chopped

2 cloves garlic, minced

2 tbsp (30 mL) all-purpose flour

1 tbsp (15 mL) curry powder

1 tbsp (15 mL) grated gingerroot (or 1 tsp/5 mL ground ginger)

1 tsp (5 mL) ground cumin

1 tsp (5 mL) fennel seeds

1 tsp (5 mL) salt

2 cups (500 mL) vegetable broth

1 cup (250 mL) water or apple juice

1 cup (250 mL) dried green lentils, picked over and rinsed

2 cups (500 mL) peeled chopped butternut squash

1 large potato, chopped into 1-inch (2.5 cm) cubes

6 cups (1.5 L) fresh spinach, washed and trimmed

½ cup (125 mL) cashews (salted or unsalted)

1 In a skillet, heat oil over medium heat. Add onion and garlic and cook for 5 minutes, or until softened and translucent. Stir in flour, curry, ginger, cumin, fennel seeds and salt; mix well.

2 Stir in broth and water; bring to a boil, scraping up bits from bottom of skillet. Transfer mixture to slow cooker stoneware.

3 Add lentils, squash and potato to slow cooker; stir to combine.

4 Cover and cook on Low for 7 to 9 hours or on High for 3 to 4 hours, until hot and bubbling.

5 Add spinach leaves; stir to combine. Cover and cook on High for 15 minutes longer, or until leaves have wilted. Spoon into individual bowls and sprinkle with cashews.

FRESH GINGERROOT

There is no need to peel gingerroot before grating. Use a standard kitchen grater with fine holes. Wrap any unused ginger in plastic wrap and freeze. Frozen gingerroot can be grated without defrosting.

TIPS

A bowlful of this curry makes a hearty meal. Serve with warm pita bread.

While cooked green lentils are available in cans, the dried variety are fast and easy to cook. It is important to pick over lentils to remove any sticks or broken pieces, then rinse and drain before using.

MOROCCAN VEGETABLE STEW

SERVES 4 TO 6 | 4- TO 6-QUART SLOW COOKER

This hearty Moroccan-inspired stew combines squash and chickpeas, lightly scented with fragrant cinnamon. It is best served over hot, fluffy couscous.

2 carrots, sliced

1 butternut squash, peeled and cut into 1-inch (2.5 cm) cubes

1 onion, chopped

1 can (19 oz/540 mL) chickpeas, drained and rinsed

1 can (19 oz/540 mL) diced tomatoes, with juices

1 cup (250 mL) vegetable broth

½ cup (125 mL) chopped pitted prunes

1 tsp (5 mL) ground cinnamon

½ tsp (2 mL) hot pepper flakes

2 tbsp (30 mL) chopped fresh parsley or cilantro

Salt and freshly ground black pepper

Hot couscous

1 In slow cooker stoneware, combine carrots, squash, onion, chickpeas, tomatoes with juices, broth, prunes, cinnamon and hot pepper flakes; stir to mix well.

2 Cover and cook on Low for 6 to 8 hours or on High for 3 to 4 hours, until all vegetables are tender.

3 Stir parsley into stew and season to taste with salt and black pepper. Serve over hot cooked couscous.

MAKE AHEAD This dish can be completely assembled the night before. Follow preparation directions and refrigerate overnight in the slow cooker stoneware. The next day, place stoneware in slow cooker and continue cooking as directed.

TIP

You can substitute chopped Medjool dates in place of the prunes. Remove the pit first before chopping.

COUSCOUS

Couscous is another name for semolina, the milled center of durum wheat. It is traditionally served with North African dishes — particularly those from Morocco, Algeria and Tunisia — and it takes less time to prepare than rice.

CHUNKY VEGETABLE PAELLA

SERVES 6 | 4- TO 6-QUART SLOW COOKER

This vegetable-rich recipe calls for saffron, an exotic herb that is worth the extra money. By adding beans to this rice dish, you get the nutritional benefit of a complete protein and a delicious, well-balanced meal.

½ tsp (2 mL) saffron threads

2 tbsp (30 mL) hot water

2 tsp (10 mL) olive oil

2 cloves garlic, minced

1 onion, finely chopped

4 stalks celery, thickly sliced

1 large red bell pepper, cut into ¾-inch (2 cm) pieces

1 large zucchini, quartered lengthwise and cut into ¾-inch (2 cm) pieces

1 can (19 oz/540 mL) fire-roasted tomatoes (see tip, below), drained

2 cups (500 mL) cooked or canned white kidney beans (see page 16), drained and rinsed

1 cup (250 mL) long-grain brown parboiled (converted) rice

1 tsp (5 mL) dried oregano

1 tsp (5 mL) Cajun seasoning (see tip, below)

½ tsp (2 mL) salt

2 cups (500 mL) vegetable broth

½ cup (125 mL) frozen peas, thawed

1 In a small bowl, combine saffron and hot water. Let steep for 10 to 15 minutes.

2 In a large nonstick skillet, heat oil over medium-high heat. Sauté garlic and onion and for about 5 minutes or until tender and translucent. Transfer to slow cooker stoneware.

3 Stir in saffron with steeping water, celery, red pepper, zucchini, tomatoes, beans, rice, oregano, Cajun seasoning, salt and broth.

4 Cover and cook on Low for 6 to 8 hours or on High for 3 to 4 hours, until liquid is absorbed and rice is fluffy.

5 Stir in peas. Cover and cook on High for 10 to 15 minutes or until heated through.

TIPS

I really like the canned tomatoes labeled "fire-roasted," which have been roasted slowly over an open fire for a great, smoky Southwestern flavor. If you can't find them, use canned diced tomatoes with chili seasonings added. If you have difficulty finding either of those, a can of plain diced tomatoes is just fine, too.

Cajun seasoning is a mix of dried herbs and seasonings available in the spice section of the supermarket. But it's easy to make your own: In a small bowl, combine 1 tbsp (15 mL) paprika and dried parsley, 1½ tsp (7 mL) garlic powder and dried thyme, ¼ tsp (1 mL) salt and ⅛ tsp (0.5 mL) cayenne pepper. Store leftovers in an airtight container in a cool, dry place for up to 1 year.

MEDITERRANEAN BARLEY SALAD

SERVES 6 AS AN ENTRÉE OR 10 AS A SIDE | 4- TO 6-QUART SLOW COOKER

A friend of mine gave me this salad from her great recipe collection, and I've adapted it to the slow cooker. It's an easy salad to pack for lunch served alongside some hummus and crackers.

1 cup (250 mL) pot barley

2 cups (500 mL) vegetable broth

3 green onions, chopped

½ red bell pepper, finely chopped

½ yellow bell pepper, finely chopped

½ cup (125 mL) drained oil-packed sun-dried tomatoes (see tip, opposite), finely chopped

1 tsp (5 mL) dried oregano

½ cup (125 mL) finely chopped fresh parsley

½ cup (125 mL) sliced kalamata olives

¼ cup (60 mL) pine nuts, toasted

¼ cup (60 mL) olive oil

¼ cup (60 mL) balsamic vinegar

Salt and freshly ground black pepper

1 In slow cooker stoneware, combine barley and broth. Cover and cook on Low for 6 to 8 hours or on High for 3 to 4 hours, until barley is tender. Fluff with a fork and let cool slightly.

2 Stir in green onions, red pepper, yellow pepper, sun-dried tomatoes, oregano, parsley, olives and pine nuts.

3 In a jar with a tight-fitting lid, combine oil and vinegar; cover and shake well. Pour over salad and toss to coat. Season to taste with salt and pepper. Serve warm or cover and refrigerate until chilled, about 2 hours. Store in an airtight container in the refrigerator for up to 5 days.

BARLEY

Barley, an important cereal grain, has had the inedible hulls removed. Pot barley is husked and coarsely ground. It is polished like pearl barley, but to a lesser extent, so the kernels are less refined and retain more of the bran layer than the pearl variety. Since pot barley kernels are not as small those of pearl barley, they take a little longer to cook. In the grocery store, you'll likely find pot barley near dried peas, lentils and beans.

TIPS

For this recipe, I use bottled sun-dried tomatoes packed in olive oil, but you can also use the packaged dried ones found in the produce section of the supermarket. To rehydrate the packaged tomatoes, simply cover them with boiling water and let soak for 30 minutes or until soft and pliable.

For added protein, add 2 cups (500 mL) cooked or canned chickpeas, white kidney beans or navy beans (see page 120), drained and rinsed, with the vegetables.

TURKISH LENTILS & COUSCOUS SALAD

SERVES 6 TO 8 | 4- TO 6-QUART SLOW COOKER, STONEWARE GREASED

Making the lentils for this salad in the slow cooker is a great way to keep your kitchen cool in the summer. Serve this alongside grilled portobello mushrooms on a bed of rice.

1½ cups (375 mL) dried brown lentils, sorted and rinsed

2½ cups (625 mL) vegetable broth

¼ cup (60 mL) white wine vinegar, divided

Salt and freshly ground black pepper

1¼ cups (310 mL) water

1 cup (250 mL) couscous

¼ cup (60 mL) olive oil, divided

2 large cloves garlic, minced

2 cups (500 mL) trimmed and chopped arugula leaves

2 cups (500 mL) cherry tomatoes, halved

1 cup (250 mL) crumbled vegan feta cheese (optional)

½ cup (125 mL) finely chopped fresh mint leaves

1 In prepared slow cooker stoneware, combine lentils and broth. Cover and cook on Low for 4 to 5 hours or on High for 3½ to 4 hours, until lentils are tender.

2 Drain any excess liquid and transfer hot lentils to a bowl. Stir in 2 tbsp (30 mL) of the vinegar. Season to taste with salt and pepper. Let cool completely, stirring occasionally.

3 Meanwhile, in a saucepan, bring water to a boil. Add couscous and ½ tsp (2 mL) salt. Remove from heat, cover and let stand for 5 minutes. Fluff with a fork and transfer to a large bowl. Stir in 1 tbsp (15 mL) of the oil. Let cool completely, stirring occasionally.

4 In a small bowl, whisk together garlic, the remaining vinegar and the remaining oil. Season to taste with salt and pepper. Stir into couscous, along with lentils.

5 Just before serving, toss in arugula, tomatoes, vegan feta (if using) and mint. Season to taste with salt and pepper.

MAKE AHEAD This dish can be partially prepared 24 hours in advance. Prepare through step 2, cover and refrigerate lentils overnight. The next day, proceed with step 3.

TIP

To grease stoneware, use a nonstick vegetable spray or use the cake pan grease available in specialty cake decorating shops or bulk food stores.

TUSCAN WHITE BEANS & KALE

SERVES 4 TO 6 | 4- TO 6-QUART SLOW COOKER

This simple combination of white kidney beans (cannellini), seasoned tomatoes and vegetables makes a perfect meatless main course. It's also terrific served cold as a salad and keeps refrigerated for three days.

1 can (19 oz/540 mL) white kidney beans, drained and rinsed, or 2 cups (500 mL) home-cooked beans (see page 16)

1 can (19 oz/540 mL) stewed tomatoes, with juices

½ cup (125 mL) vegetable broth

1 stalk celery, finely chopped

1 onion, finely chopped

2 cloves garlic, minced

2 bay leaves

2 tbsp (30 mL) olive oil

½ tsp (2 mL) dried sage

½ tsp (2 mL) dried rosemary, crumbled

2 tbsp (30 mL) dry red wine

1 cup (250 mL) chopped kale

1 In slow cooker stoneware, combine beans, tomatoes, broth, celery, onion, garlic, bay leaves, olive oil, sage and rosemary.

2 Cover and cook on Low for 6 to 10 hours or on High for 3 to 4 hours, until hot and bubbling.

3 Stir in wine and kale. Cover and let stand for 5 minutes to wilt kale leaves. Discard bay leaves.

MAKE AHEAD This dish can be assembled up to 24 hours before cooking. Refrigerate overnight in slow cooker stoneware. The next day, place stoneware in slow cooker and continue to cook as directed.

TIP

Kale is a dark green, leafy vegetable that is a great source of fiber and many essential nutrients. Remove the stems and any tough veins from the leaves before using.

FOOTBALL-STYLE BAKED BEANS

SERVES 8 TO 10 | 4- TO 6-QUART SLOW COOKER

Infamous for brutally cold late-fall temperatures, Green Bay, Wisconsin, is also famous for its football field and tailgate parties. Although fans huddle around grills in boots and parkas, it's still all about the food. A spinoff from traditional baked beans, this hot and hearty combination also goes well with grilled vegan sausage.

1 tbsp (15 mL) vegetable oil

1 large onion, finely chopped

1 can (19 oz/540 mL) white kidney beans, drained and rinsed, or 2 cups (500 mL) home-cooked beans (see page 16)

1 can (19 oz/540 mL) red kidney beans, drained and rinsed, or 2 cups (500 mL) home-cooked beans (see page 16)

1 can (19 oz/540 mL) chickpeas, drained and rinsed, or 2 cups (500 mL) home-cooked chickpeas (see page 16)

1 can (7½ oz/221 mL) tomato sauce

½ cup (125 mL) ketchup

2 tbsp (30 mL) packed brown sugar

2 tsp (10 mL) prepared mustard

2 cups (500 mL) frozen green beans, thawed

1 In a large nonstick skillet, heat oil over medium-high heat. Add onion and cook, stirring occasionally, for 5 minutes, or until tender. Transfer onion to slow cooker stoneware.

2 Add white and red kidney beans, chickpeas, tomato sauce, ketchup, brown sugar and mustard to slow cooker; stir to combine.

3 Cover and cook on Low for 6 to 10 hours or on High for 3 to 4 hours, until hot and bubbling.

4 Add green beans. Cover and cook on High for 20 to 30 minutes longer, or until green beans are heated through.

TIP

Although you can use canned beans in this recipe, home-cooked dried beans are not only economical, they tend to be better tasting.

HOT CURRIED BEANS

SERVES 6 | 4- TO 6-QUART SLOW COOKER

This bean dish — perfect as a side dish or on its own for a potluck — is a real hit with my vegetarian daughter, Darcy, who loves the combination of beans, crunchy apples and sweet raisins. She is not a cilantro fan, but my husband and I enjoy a sprinkling of cilantro on top. The chutney lends some sweetness, with a little heat, while the nuts add a nice crunch.

1 lb (500 g) dried red kidney beans (about 2 cups/500 mL), sorted, rinsed and soaked (see page 16)

1 onion, sliced

8 oz (250 g) button mushrooms, sliced

½ cup (125 mL) golden raisins

1 tbsp (15 mL) curry powder

½ tsp (2 mL) freshly ground black pepper

1½ cups (375 mL) vegetable broth

¾ cup (175 mL) water

1 large red or green apple, chopped

Hot cooked couscous

Mango chutney

Chopped toasted almonds (see tip, below)

1 In slow cooker stoneware, combine soaked beans, onion, mushrooms, raisins, curry powder, pepper, broth and water.

2 Cover and cook on Low for 4 to 6 hours or until beans are tender. Stir in apples and cook for 15 minutes.

3 Spoon beans over couscous, top each serving with a dollop of chutney and sprinkle with almonds.

TIP

To toast almonds, spread nuts in a single layer in a shallow baking pan or rimmed baking sheet. Bake in a 350°F (180°C) oven, stirring or shaking once or twice, for 5 to 10 minutes or until golden brown and fragrant.

SIDES

CHEDDAR SCALLOPED POTATOES

SERVES 6 | 4- TO 6-QUART SLOW COOKER, STONEWARE GREASED

This has got to be everyone's favorite potato dish. It goes well with ham, pork, chicken or turkey. My friend (and die-hard potato lover) Kathy Shortt was my principal taste-tester for this recipe. She gave it a perfect 10!

6 potatoes, peeled and sliced

1 onion, sliced

¼ cup (60 mL) celery leaves

1 tbsp (15 mL) dried parsley

2 tbsp (30 mL) butter or margarine, melted

¼ cup (60 mL) all-purpose flour

1 tsp (5 mL) salt

½ tsp (2 mL) freshly ground black pepper

1 can (12 oz/354 mL) evaporated milk

1 cup (250 mL) shredded Cheddar cheese

½ tsp (2 mL) paprika

1 Layer potato slices and onion in prepared slow cooker stoneware.

2 In a blender or food processor, combine celery leaves, parsley, melted butter, flour, salt, pepper, evaporated milk and Cheddar cheese. Process for 1 minute, or until mixture is smooth. Pour over potatoes and onions; sprinkle with paprika.

3 Cover and cook on Low for 6 to 8 hours or on High for 3 to 4 hours, until potatoes are tender and heated through.

MAKE AHEAD This dish can be prepared a day ahead. Combine liquid ingredients and pour over potato and onion slices. Cover and refrigerate for up to 24 hours. Bake as directed.

TIP

If you don't have a blender or food processor, finely chop all ingredients for the milk sauce. Pour over potatoes and continue as directed.

SPICED SWEET POTATOES

SERVES 4 TO 6 | 4- TO 6-QUART SLOW COOKER

If I have one guilty food pleasure, it is sweet potato fries. Whenever I see them on a restaurant menu, I order a side. This version is a great combination of savory and sweet, it's a lot healthier than deep-fried potatoes, and it's perfect for a summer menu with grilled chicken or fish — and you won't heat up the kitchen.

2¼ lbs (1.125 kg) sweet potatoes (about 5)

2 tbsp (30 mL) olive oil

1 tbsp (15 mL) freshly squeezed lime juice

1 tsp (5 mL) chili powder

½ tsp (2 mL) ground cumin

½ tsp (2 mL) salt

¼ tsp (1 mL) ground cinnamon

1 Peel sweet potatoes and cut into 2-inch (5 cm) long, ½-inch (1 cm) thick sticks.

2 In slow cooker stoneware, toss together sweet potatoes, oil, lime juice, chili powder, cumin, salt and cinnamon.

3 Cover and cook on Low for about 3 hours or until sweet potatoes are tender but still hold their shape. Drain off any remaining liquid before serving.

TIP

To get the most juice from a lime, let it warm to room temperature, then roll it on the counter, pressing down with the palm of your hand, before squeezing it. Or microwave a whole lime on High for 30 seconds, then roll, cut and squeeze it. Juice can be frozen in ice cube trays, then kept in the freezer in sealable plastic bags for later use. Zest can also be wrapped and frozen for later use.

WARM CAESAR POTATO SALAD

SERVES 6 TO 8 | 4- TO 6-QUART SLOW COOKER

At restaurants, Caesar salad is requested more than any other. Here's a twist on that old favorite: toss the creamy salad dressing on hot, braised potatoes for an irresistibly delicious side dish.

2 lbs (1 kg) red or white mini potatoes

1 onion, chopped

2 tbsp (30 mL) olive oil

½ tsp (2 mL) salt

¼ tsp (1 mL) freshly ground black pepper

2 tbsp (30 mL) water

6 slices bacon, cooked crisp and crumbled

3 green onions, sliced

2 cloves garlic, minced

½ cup (125 mL) freshly grated Parmesan cheese

½ cup (125 mL) creamy Caesar salad dressing

¼ cup (60 mL) chopped fresh basil

1 In slow cooker stoneware, combine potatoes, onion, oil, salt, pepper and water.

2 Cover and cook on Low for 3 to 3½ hours or until potatoes are tender.

3 Discard cooking liquid and transfer potato mixture to a large bowl. Add bacon, green onions, garlic, cheese and dressing; toss to coat. Sprinkle with basil and serve warm.

MAKE AHEAD This dish can be fully prepared up to 2 days in advance. Cover and refrigerate. Serve cold or let warm to room temperature.

TIP

If mini potatoes are not available, use larger ones cut into quarters.

PARMESAN CHEESE

Authentic Parmesan cheese (Parmigiano-Reggiano) is expensive, but its flavor is certainly worth the price. Well-wrapped in the refrigerator, a block keeps for months, and it goes a long way when you freshly grate it as you need it. Grated versions found on supermarket shelves have a soapy, salty taste that can't compare with freshly grated Parmesan.

CREAMY BLUE CHEESE GRITS

SERVES 6 TO 8 | 3- TO 4-QUART SLOW COOKER

When we travel south to the Sunshine State, I get my fill of grits wherever I can. When I asked my friend Kristine in Knoxville, Tennessee, to send me a recipe, she turned to her friend Suzanne. According to Suzanne, grits is an acronym for Girls Raised in the South. No wonder I love them so much! Blue cheese grits are great served alongside a grilled steak.

1 cup (250 mL) grits or coarse cornmeal

¼ cup (60 mL) butter

1 tsp (5 mL) coarse salt

5 cups (1.25 mL) water

¼ cup (60 mL) crumbled blue cheese

¼ cup (60 mL) sour cream

1 In slow cooker stoneware, combine grits, butter, salt and 5 cups (1.25 L) water.

2 Cover and cook on Low for 4 to 5 hours or on High for 2 to $2\frac{1}{2}$ hours, until thickened.

3 Stir in cheese and sour cream. Serve immediately.

VARIATION

If you prefer something more mainstream, use 1 cup (250 mL) shredded Cheddar, smoked Gouda or Monterey Jack cheese instead of the blue cheese.

GRITS

Grits are dried corn kernels ground fine, medium or coarse. They are often simmered with water or milk until fairly thick. Quick grits (a very fine grind that has been presteamed) are available in supermarkets, but don't use them in this recipe. If you have difficulty finding grits, look for coarse or stone-ground cornmeal in a specialty, bulk food or health food store.

PERFECT SOUTHERN GREENS

SERVES 6 TO 8 | 4- TO 6-QUART SLOW COOKER

This recipe yields the best-tasting greens I have ever eaten. It has the potential to convert those who thing they don't like greens.

1 lb (500 g) mild Italian sausage, casings removed

8 cups (2 L) kale, tough ribs and stems removed, torn into 2-inch (5 cm) pieces

1 tsp (5 mL) salt

½ tsp (2 mL) freshly ground black pepper

2 cups (500 mL) water

2 to 3 tsp (10 to 15 mL) red wine vinegar (optional)

1 In a large skillet, cook sausage over medium-high heat, breaking it up with the back of a wooden spoon, for about 6 to 8 minutes or until browned. Using a slotted spoon, transfer to slow cooker stoneware. Stir in kale, salt, pepper and water.

2 Cover and cook on Low for 6 hours or on High for 3 hours, until kale is tender. Stir in vinegar (if using). Serve hot.

TIPS

Blanching the kale before adding it to the slow cooker can help remove some of its natural bitterness. Add torn greens to a pot of boiling salted water and cook for 4 to 5 minutes. Drain well. This will reduce the cooking time to 4 hours on Low or 2 hours on High.

You can also substitute beet, collard or mustard greens for the kale.

KALE

A member of the cabbage family, kale has beautiful dark green, curly leaves. It has been dubbed a "superfood" for its cancer-fighting phytonutrients. Although it can be found year-round in the supermarket, it is in season from the middle of winter through the beginning of spring, a time when quality green foods can otherwise be difficult to find.

TANGY RED CABBAGE WITH APPLES

SERVES 6 | 4- TO 6-QUART SLOW COOKER

This is a great side dish for any meal, especially a chicken, pork or sausage entrée.

1 medium head red cabbage, shredded (about 10 cups/2.5 L)

2 Granny Smith apples, peeled and thinly sliced

1 onion, sliced

¼ cup (60 mL) red wine vinegar

¼ cup (60 mL) packed brown sugar

2 tbsp (30 mL) butter or margarine

½ cup (125 mL) water

1 tsp (5 mL) salt

1 tsp (5 mL) celery seed

½ tsp (2 mL) freshly ground black pepper

1 In slow cooker stoneware, toss together cabbage, apples and onion slices.

2 In a saucepan, over medium-high heat, combine vinegar, brown sugar, butter, water, salt, celery seed and pepper. Bring mixture to a boil, reduce heat and simmer for 1 minute, or until butter is melted and sugar is dissolved. Pour over cabbage mixture in slow cooker.

3 Cover and cook on Low for 4 to 6 hours, or until cabbage is tender.

TIPS

Don't worry about being too precise with the cooking time in this recipe — the cabbage can steam away on Low all day.

If you are using a food processor to shred the cabbage, use it also for the onions and apples; it will save you a lot of time.

Leftover cabbage can be frozen until needed. Pack in freezer-safe containers and store for up to 3 months. To reheat, microwave on High until hot.

Adjust the sugar and vinegar to suit your taste.

The vinegar not only adds flavor, but helps preserve the red color of the cabbage.

COUNTRY-STYLE SAGE & BREAD STUFFING

SERVES 10 TO 12 | 4- TO 6-QUART SLOW COOKER

Is it stuffing or dressing? Technically, it's stuffing when it's baked inside the bird and dressing when it's not. Whichever the case, stuffing cooked inside the slow cooker is moist, delicious and a lot easier to get out!

½ cup (125 mL) butter

2 onions, finely chopped

2 stalks celery, finely chopped

½ cup (125 mL) finely chopped fresh parsley

1½ tsp (7 mL) dried rosemary, crumbled

1½ tsp (7 mL) dried thyme

1½ tsp (7 mL) dried marjoram

1½ tsp (7 mL) dried sage

1½ tsp (7 mL) salt

½ tsp (2 mL) ground nutmeg

½ tsp (2 mL) freshly ground black pepper

1 loaf day-old sourdough bread, cut into ½-inch (1 cm) cubes (about 10 cups/2.5 L)

1½ cups (375 mL) chicken, turkey or vegetable broth

1 In a large nonstick skillet, heat butter over medium-high heat. Add onions and celery and cook, stirring occasionally, for about 10 minutes, or until onions are softened. Add parsley, rosemary, thyme, marjoram, sage, salt, nutmeg and pepper. Cook, stirring, for 1 minute.

2 Place bread cubes in a large bowl and add onion mixture; stir to combine. Slowly add broth, tossing gently to moisten. Transfer to slow cooker stoneware.

3 Cover and cook on High for 1 hour. Reduce heat to Low and cook for 2 to 3 hours longer, or until heated through. (The slow cooker will keep the stuffing at serving temperature. Keep on Low for up to 3 hours after stuffing is cooked.)

VARIATIONS

Dried Fruit Stuffing: Add 1 cup (250 mL) chopped dried fruit such as cranberries, apples, raisins and currants to stuffing and stir in for last hour of cooking.

Mushroom Stuffing: In a large skillet, melt ¼ cup (60 mL) butter over medium heat. Add 1½ lbs (750 g) sliced mushrooms and cook, stirring often, for 10 to 12 minutes, or until liquid has evaporated and mushrooms are beginning to brown. Stir cooked mushrooms into stuffing for last hour of cooking.

CHORIZO & PECAN CORNBREAD STUFFING

SERVES 10 | 6- TO 8-QUART SLOW COOKER, STONEWARE GREASED

Sausage is a wonderful addition to stuffing because the meat is so highly seasoned. This recipe has a nice Southwestern twist, and using the slow cooker makes it fuss-free.

1 lb (500 g) fresh chorizo sausage, casings removed

3 stalks celery, finely chopped

1 large onion, finely chopped

½ cup (125 mL) dry white wine

2 eggs, beaten

12 cups (3 L) cubed cornbread (see recipe, opposite)

3 tbsp (45 mL) finely chopped fresh sage

½ tsp (2 mL) salt

¼ tsp (1 mL) freshly ground black pepper

1½ cups (375 mL) hot chicken broth

2 tbsp (30 mL) melted butter

1½ cups (375 mL) coarsely chopped pecans, toasted (see box, opposite)

1 In a large nonstick skillet, cook sausage over medium-high heat, breaking it up with the back of a wooden spoon, for 5 to 7 minutes or until starting to brown. Add celery and onion; sauté for about 5 minutes or until softened. Add wine and boil, stirring, for 3 to 5 minutes or until evaporated. Transfer to a large bowl.

2 Gently toss in eggs, cornbread, sage, salt and pepper (cornbread will break down into smaller pieces). The sausage mixture should be moist but not soggy; if necessary, add up to ½ cup (125 mL) of the hot broth. Transfer to prepared slow cooker stoneware.

3 Combine the remaining broth and butter. Drizzle over sausage mixture.

4 Cover and cook on Low for 3 hours or until heated through. Gently stir in pecans. (The stuffing will hold on Low or Warm for up to 1 hour before serving.)

QUICK AND EASY CORNBREAD

- Preheat oven to 425°F (220°C)
- 9-inch (23 cm) square glass baking dish

½ cup (125 mL) butter, divided

1½ cups (375 mL) cornmeal

1½ cups (375 mL) all-purpose flour

¼ cup (60 mL) granulated sugar

2 tsp (10 mL) baking soda

2 tsp (10 mL) salt

3 eggs

2½ cups (625 mL) buttermilk

1 Spread 2 tbsp (30 mL) of the butter over bottom and sides of baking dish. Melt the remaining butter. Set aside.

2 In a bowl, whisk together cornmeal, flour, sugar, baking soda and salt. In another bowl, whisk together eggs, buttermilk and melted butter. Add cornmeal mixture to buttermilk mixture and stir just until moistened (do not overmix). Spread in prepared baking dish.

3 Bake in preheated oven for 15 to 20 minutes or until golden and a tester inserted in the center comes out clean. Let cool in dish on a wire rack for 10 minutes before slicing.

TIP

To grease stoneware, use a nonstick vegetable spray or use the cake pan grease available in specialty cake decorating shops or bulk food stores.

TOASTING NUTS

Toasting nuts enhances their flavor and texture. Spread nuts on a baking sheet. Toast in a 350°F (160°C) oven for 5 to 7 minutes, or until golden brown, stirring occasionally.

DESSERTS

CARMELIZED BANANA SPLIT

SERVES 4, PLUS EXTRA SAUCE | 1- TO 3-QUART SLOW COOKER OR SLOW COOKER WARMER

With its warm, gooey goodness, this dessert will bring to mind those lazy days of summer. You'll have some sauce left over, which is handy because — I assure you — you'll be in the mood to have this again the next night, if not sooner!

WARM RASPBERRY CHOCOLATE SAUCE

1 lb (500 g) bittersweet or semisweet chocolate, chopped

1 cup (250 mL) heavy or whipping (35%) cream

$\frac{1}{3}$ cup (75 mL) seedless raspberry jam

1 tsp (5 mL) vanilla extract

BANANA SPLITS

3 tbsp (45 mL) butter

3 firm ripe bananas, cut diagonally into $\frac{1}{2}$-inch (1 cm) slices

$\frac{1}{4}$ cup (60 mL) lightly packed brown sugar

Cinnamon or vanilla ice cream

$\frac{1}{2}$ cup (125 mL) chopped walnuts, toasted (see box, page 177)

1 SAUCE: In slow cooker stoneware, combine chocolate, cream and jam. Cover and cook on Low for $1\frac{1}{2}$ to 2 hours, stirring two or three times, until chocolate is melted and sauce is smooth and hot. Whisk in vanilla.

2 BANANA SPLITS: In a large, heavy skillet, melt butter over medium heat. Add bananas in a single layer and sprinkle with brown sugar. Increase heat to medium-high and cook, shaking skillet occasionally and gently turning bananas once, for 3 to 4 minutes or until sugar is caramelized.

3 Divide bananas among individual serving bowls. Top with scoops of ice cream, drizzle with sauce and sprinkle with walnuts.

TIP

To store the extra sauce, transfer it to an airtight container and refrigerate for up to 2 weeks. To serve warm, reheat in the microwave on Medium (50%) power or in a saucepan over low heat.

CARAMEL PEACHES

SERVES 4 TO 6 | 4- TO 6-QUART SLOW COOKER

This easy-to-make dessert combines fresh juicy peaches with a sweet butterscotch sauce. It's the perfect dish to whip together when peaches are in season.

6 peaches, peeled and sliced, or 3 cans (each 14 oz/398 mL) peach halves, drained and sliced

2 tsp (10 mL) freshly squeezed lemon juice

1 cup (250 mL) packed brown sugar

3 tbsp (45 mL) melted butter or margarine

¼ cup (60 mL) whipping (35%) cream

½ tsp (2 mL) ground cinnamon

Vanilla ice cream (optional)

1 In a bowl, toss together peach slices and lemon juice.

2 In slow cooker stoneware, combine brown sugar, butter, cream and cinnamon; mix well. Add peach slices and toss to coat with brown sugar mixture.

3 Cover and cook on Low for 4 to 6 hours, until fruit is bubbling.

4 If desired, serve over vanilla ice cream.

TIPS

Serve these peaches over vanilla ice cream or simply enjoy them on their own. You can substitute sliced apples for the peaches.

To quickly ripen fresh peaches, place in a brown paper bag and let stand overnight at room temperature.

To peel peaches, plunge in boiling water for 30 seconds to loosen skin and quickly plunge into cold water. Skin should easily slip off.

CREAMY CARAMEL BLONDIES

SERVES 4 TO 6 | 4- TO 6-QUART SLOW COOKER

My son, Jack, and I are caramel and butterscotch fanatics! Blondies are often described as brownies without chocolate, which I find silly: blondies have their own unique, delicious personality. While brownies depend on chocolate for their flavor, with blondies it's all about the brown sugar. This tasty dessert combines a cake top over a creamy caramel sauce. Be sure to serve with a big scoop of vanilla ice cream.

1 cup (250 mL) all-purpose flour

1 tsp (5 mL) baking powder

½ tsp (2 mL) salt

1 cup (250 mL) packed brown sugar, divided

¼ cup (60 mL) butter, softened

1 tsp (5 mL) vanilla extract

½ cup (125 mL) milk

½ cup (125 mL) soft caramels, wrappers removed

1 cup (250 mL) boiling water

1 In a bowl, combine flour, baking powder and salt.

2 In another bowl, using an electric mixer, beat half the brown sugar and butter until creamy. Stir in vanilla. Add flour mixture alternately with milk, making three additions of each and beating well after each addition. Stir in caramels. Spread batter evenly in slow cooker stoneware.

3 In a glass measuring cup, combine the remaining brown sugar and boiling water, stirring until sugar is dissolved. Pour evenly over batter.

4 Cover and cook on High for 2½ to 3 hours or until a toothpick inserted in the center comes out clean.

TIP
It is best to use individually wrapped soft caramels, but you can substitute ½ cup (125 mL) butterscotch chips.

MEXICAN CHOCOLATE BREAD PUDDING

SERVES 6 TO 8 | 4- TO 6-QUART SLOW COOKER, STONEWARE GREASED

This Mexican dessert, called capirotadas, is traditionally served during Lent. It is full of texture and flavor, and with a few savory garnishes, such as sour cream or thin slices of aged Cheddar or Monterey Jack cheese, it also makes a wonderful breakfast or brunch dish.

2 cups (500 mL) light (5%) cream

4 oz (125 g) unsweetened chocolate, coarsely chopped

2 eggs, beaten

½ cup (125 mL) packed brown sugar

¾ tsp (3 mL) ground cinnamon

½ tsp (2 mL) ground allspice

⅛ tsp (0.5 mL) salt

1 tsp (5 mL) vanilla extract

½ cup (125 mL) dried currants

4 thick slices stale egg bread or challah, crusts removed, cut into 1-inch (2.5 cm) cubes (about 4 cups/2 L)

⅓ cup (75 mL) slivered almonds

Sour cream (optional)

1 In a heavy saucepan, bring cream to a simmer over medium heat. Remove from heat. Add chocolate and let stand for 2 to 3 minutes. Stir until chocolate is melted. Let cool slightly.

2 In a large bowl, whisk together eggs, brown sugar, cinnamon, allspice, salt and vanilla. Stir in currants. Stir in cream mixture. Gently fold in bread cubes. Pour into prepared slow cooker stoneware. Sprinkle evenly with almonds.

3 Cover and cook on High for 3 to 4 hours or until a tester inserted in the center comes out clean.

4 Serve warm or chilled. Top each serving with generous dollop of sour cream, if desired.

MAKE AHEAD This dish can be assembled up to 24 hours in advance. Prepare through step 2, cover and refrigerate. When ready to cook, place stoneware in slow cooker and proceed with step 3.

TIPS

Regardless of which bread you use, it's important that it is stale. The staler the bread, the more readily it absorbs the custard mixture and the more tender and flavorful the pudding will be. I often cube leftover bread, then leave it out, uncovered, to dry.

Challah (pronounced HAH-lah) is a traditional Jewish bread made with eggs, yeast, flour and water. It has a distinct yellow interior because of the yolks used to make it. Challah is one of the best breads to use for bread pudding, because you can easily cut it into thick slices and it absorbs the egg mixture quickly.

RHUBARB BLUEBERRY PUDDING CAKE

SERVES 6 TO 8 | 4- TO 6-QUART SLOW COOKER, STONEWARE GREASED

Stewed blueberries and rhubarb topped with a steamed moist cake layer make a wonderful old-fashioned dessert. I like to make this with the rhubarb from my garden. I freeze it and bring out as much as I need so it's ready at hand for special recipes such as this one.

1 cup (250 mL) chopped fresh or frozen rhubarb

2 cups (500 mL) fresh or frozen blueberries

1/4 cup (60 mL) butter

1 1/4 cups (310 mL) granulated sugar, divided

3/4 cup (175 mL) all-purpose flour

1 tsp (5 mL) baking powder

1/2 tsp (2 mL) ground cinnamon

1/4 tsp (1 mL) ground nutmeg

Pinch salt

1/2 cup (125 mL) milk

1 tbsp (15 mL) cornstarch

1 tsp (5 mL) grated orange zest

1/2 cup (125 mL) freshly squeezed orange juice

Whipped cream (optional)

1 Place rhubarb and blueberries in prepared slow cooker stoneware.

2 In a bowl, cream together butter and 3/4 cup (175 mL) of the granulated sugar.

3 In another bowl, combine flour, baking powder, cinnamon, nutmeg and salt. Add to butter mixture alternately with milk. Spread over fruit in slow cooker.

4 In a small saucepan, combine cornstarch, remaining 1/2 cup (125 mL) granulated sugar and orange zest. Stir in orange juice. Bring to a boil over medium-high heat; cook, stirring constantly, until slightly thickened. Remove from heat and pour over batter in slow cooker.

5 Cover and cook on High for 2 to 3 hours, or until top is golden and fruit is bubbly. Serve warm with dollops of whipped cream, if desired.

TIP

If fresh rhubarb or blue-berries are unavailable, use frozen. There is no need to thaw them first.

WARM CHOCOLATE LAVA CAKE

SERVES 8 | 3- TO 4-QUART SLOW COOKER, STONEWARE GREASED

This decadent dessert is supremely rich and incredibly delicious. It originally developed from a kitchen error: the chef simply had no more time to bake the cake, so he called it a "lava" cake. Sometimes less time is a delicious thing!

2 cups (500 mL) semisweet chocolate chips

¾ cup (175 mL) butter, cut into cubes

6 eggs

⅔ cup (150 mL) granulated sugar

2 tsp (10 mL) vanilla extract

2 tbsp (30 mL) all-purpose flour

Coffee or vanilla ice cream

1 In a large microwave-safe glass bowl or an 8-cup (2 L) glass measuring cup, combine chocolate chips and butter. Microwave on Medium (50%) for $2\frac{1}{2}$ to 3 minutes, stirring every minute, until melted and smooth.

2 Whisk in eggs, sugar and vanilla until smooth. Whisk in flour until blended and smooth. Spread evenly in prepared slow cooker stoneware.

3 Cover and cook on High for 2 to $2\frac{1}{2}$ hours or until edges are set but center is slightly runny. Serve immediately with ice cream.

TIPS

Most recipes use large eggs. If a recipe doesn't specify a size, assume you need large.

Do not be tempted to use the Low setting to bake this cake. It requires high heat to bake properly.

INDEX

Library and Archives Canada Cataloguing in Publication
Title: Today's everyday slow cooker : 100 easy & delicious recipes / Donna-Marie Pye.
Other titles: Slow cooker
Names: Pye, Donna-Marie, author.
Identifiers: Canadiana 20200275208 | ISBN 9780778806769 (softcover)
Subjects: LCSH: Electric cooking, Slow. | LCGFT: Cookbooks.
Classification: LCC TX827 .P94 2021 | DDC 641.5/884—dc23